Social
Stratification
and
Deviant
Behavior

John P. Hewitt

York University

Social Stratification and Deviant Behavior

Random House   New York

For Myrna, Beth, and Gary

Preface

The aim of this book is to introduce a large and important topic: the relationship between what is ordinarily called "deviant behavior" and social inequalities of power, prestige, and property. Empirical connections between inequality and deviance are usually—though not always—easily established. It is more difficult, however, to isolate the causal mechanisms. In this analysis I shall deal in detail with one such causal mechanism: self-esteem.

I begin by discussing the meaning of deviant behavior and then go on to analyze social stratification and to construct a set of attendant propositions for demonstration. Then I discuss self-esteem as an explanatory variable and formulate relevant propositions. Successive chapters deal with deviant behavior and self-esteem among juvenile, and adult, members of the lower and middle social strata of American society. The concluding chapter raises a series of important questions about social inequality and deviant behavior.

I do not claim that self-esteem is the sole social-psychological variable relevant to the explanation of deviant (or even non-deviant) behavior. But I have chosen to emphasize it because it seems crucial and also because of the less than systematic treatment it has received in the theoretical and empirical literature of sociology. Although other variables are clearly important too, I believe it is necessary and desirable to limit treatment of them in this analysis.

I have tried to elaborate and illustrate a sociological theory that I believe holds great promise for the understanding of human behavior. The student will profit most from it if he reads the book in conjunction with empirical studies of deviant behavior and if he seeks to relate this theory to other theories of behavior and to himself.

I am deeply indebted to Marvin Bressler for his expert guidance while I was writing this book; my personal and intellectual debt to Melvin Tumin is too great to describe or repay here. My former students at Oberlin College and my colleagues there and at York University have provided stimulating and rewarding contexts in which to write and think. The editorial staff of Random House has helped significantly to make this book more readable and understandable. My wife, Myrna Livingston Hewitt, knows best the magnitude of this task and her own contributions to its completion.

Toronto, Ontario   J. P. H.
December, 1969

Contents

Social
Stratification
and
Deviant
Behavior

Analytical Models of Social Stratification and Deviant Behavior

1

Before we take up the intricacies of deviant behavior, some brief comments on our overall approach are in order. Our objective is to develop a theory capable of accounting for the diverse empirical findings that link social inequality and deviant behavior, particularly in American society. The subject of this book is the influence of structured social inequalities in generating deviant behavior. Accordingly, in this chapter and the next we shall seek answers to three important questions. First, what is deviant behavior? From what or whose norms does such behavior deviate, and who designates it as deviant? Second, what is a system of social stratification, how does it operate, and what particular social inequalities does it comprise? Third, given that deviant behavior and social stratification are linked empirically, what theory best explains the connections? In this chapter we shall take up the first two questions. In the next chapter we shall begin to treat the third.

The ideal goal is to design a set of concepts—and propositions that will permit us to deduce the already observed empirical links between stratification variables (like income, education, and occupation) and deviant behavior. This task is one of the most pressing and difficult now facing the social sciences.

Of course, it is not difficult merely to set up a series of premises in order to explain a social phenomenon. As participants in systems of social action we all evolve "theories" to account for the behavior of others. As scientific observers we do the same, even in the act of observation. ["Laws"] deductive nomological explanations of behavior are extraordinarily easy to deduce from isolated instances.[1] The difficulties arise when these explanations must meet the rigorous test of broad-scale observation: Not only must conclusions follow from premises; the premises themselves must be valid. Furthermore, the presented theory must be able to generate new deductions that can in turn be validated by empirical evidence. The possibilities of error are great. We can make erroneous observations, thus creating false premises from which we can make still further deductions, which may be partly true and partly false. Or we can make accurate observations but create false explanations, from which further deductions can be made, some of which may be partly true and partly false. Such difficulties can be compounded in a number of ways: first, through insufficient evidence to test all possible deductions from a single theory; second, through overlooking some possible deductions from a set of premises; third, through the general imprecision of social-scientific data and methods compared to those of the natural sciences; and, fourth, through reliance on verbal explanations, which are subject to all the imprecision and ambiguity of language.

It might seem that before attempting to formulate theory we ought first to develop more precise measuring techniques capable of producing more precise, even mathematically precise, conclusions, so that we could at least control the implications of our statements. In science, however, improvements in methods and measurements often go hand in hand with the refinement of theories, and it is frequently difficult to determine which problems to attack first. Science works best, we believe, when it maintains a "no holds barred" attitude toward investigation of any problem. We have chosen to attempt the construction of an explanatory theory on the grounds that we shall simultaneously incorporate what evidence has already accumulated and learn the areas in which we are still empirically and methodologically weak.

So much for introductory remarks. Our first problem is to define and analyze deviant behavior.

Deviant Behavior

Just as we must understand how society is organized before we can explain how it becomes disorganized, so we must first explore nondeviant behavior, in order to achieve an adequate understanding of deviant behavior. And the question of deviant behavior does indeed rest upon the question of social control, of the social forces that cause people to behave in given ways. We shall distinguish three mechanisms of behavioral motivation and control, one or more of which can be discerned in any behavior.

Normative Regulation of Behavior

The first mechanism can be called "normative regulation of behavior." In any society a significant portion of all social action is regulated by the individual's development of commitment to social norms. A norm is a standard or principle of conduct viewed as right and binding by most of those who adhere to it in their behavior. Norms specify behavior that is expected (they prescribe) and behavior that is to be avoided (they proscribe). They are frequently based on a more general set of values. We speak of *commitment* to social norms when a person behaves in accord with a norm and displays his assent to its validity and rightness.[2] This definition of commitment is based on a fourfold classification type of behavior, as indicated in Table 1. Some behavior is normative, yet the individual does not accept the validity of the norms to which his behavior conforms. In other cases, individuals accept the validity of norms but do not behave accordingly. Finally, some behavior is marked by total absence of commitment: The individual neither behaves normatively nor regards the norms as valid.

Committed behavior frequently reflects the internalization of norms. We say that a norm is "internalized" when it becomes so thoroughly incorporated into the self that it produces a persistent predisposition in behavior, that obeying the norm becomes rewarding in itself, and that violation of it arouses guilt. For example, a businessman who has internalized a norm that work is always preferable to idleness will very likely feel guilty about taking a holiday or even an extra five minutes for coffee.

Table 1: Types of Behavior and Their Control

Person's Orientation to Norms

	PERSON ASSENTS TO VALIDITY OF THE NORMS	PERSON DOES NOT ASSENT TO VALIDITY OF THE NORMS
BEHAVIOR IS NORMATIVE:	*Full commitment:* behavior is controlled and motivated by person's orientation to the norms; other factors, such as group supports, may also be involved in keeping behavior in line with norms.	*Absent commitment:* the person's behavior is kept in line with norms only by other factors, such as group coercion, which overcome his tendency not to behave normatively.
BEHAVIOR IS NOT NORMATIVE:	*Reduced commitment:* behavior is kept from being normative by other factors that overcome his desire to behave normatively.	*Absent commitment:* explanation of person's behavior must seek factors other than normative ones, such as responses to coercion or to various situational constraints.

We cannot say that all committed behavior involves internalization of norms, however, or that internalization of norms guarantees normative behavior. These points deserve elaboration. First, committed behavior does not necessarily reflect internalized norms. For example, a college professor may believe that he should attend faculty meetings, and he may actually attend most of them. But, if absence does not arouse guilt in him, he has not internalized the norm requiring attendance. It has not been incorporated into his self nor is attendance in itself rewarding. But his actual behavior does suggest that the professor performs certain duties to earn approval from his colleagues and thus to avoid any sense of shame before them. The main point is that acceptance of the validity of a norm need not involve its internalization. Some committed behavior—which is normative and which reflects the individual's belief that his behavior is right and proper—is also governed by the social group, which demands conformity and whose unfavorable response to deviance produces shame in the violator. We argue that the paired concepts of group support and shame deserve a theoretical status equal to that of internalization and guilt. When internalized norms are violated, the internal phenomenon of guilt is aroused, regardless of whether or not such violations are socially condemned. When an individual violates a norm that he supports, but that he has not internalized, the social phenomenon of shame is produced if his violation is noticed and condemned by others.[3] Thus, the businessman in our example is his own moral censor, but the professor feels embarrassed only when his colleagues register disapproval.

Even where a norm has been internalized, there may be circumstances in which a person cannot live up to it—for example, in cases where other norms that he has internalized conflict with the norm in question. Where a norm has *not* been internalized, there is an even greater chance that the person may not be able to live up to it. The regulation of behavior thus involves both personal and social controls. This point is relevant to our third category of behavior, in which acceptance, even internalization, of a norm is not in itself sufficient to guarantee normative behavior. People can—and not infrequently do—violate the very norms whose validity they voluntarily support. Unless this point is recognized we shall be tempted to assume mistakenly that an individual's behavior is an automatic process that requires only development of positive orientations toward norms.

Two conditions must be met for an individual's behavior to be normative. One condition is personal, the other social. Whether or not the norm in question is internalized, the individual must regard it as valid and important enough to follow. The professor must believe it proper to attend faculty meetings, and the businessman must think it right to work so hard. On the other hand, there must also be some level of group support for normative performance. That is, the group must reward the person for behavior in accordance with its norms, and the individual must be in some way related to the group either as a member or as a nonmember who nevertheless keys his behavior to it. We say therefore that the normative regulation of behavior requires the existence either of personal controls (through attachment to group norms) or social controls (through attachment to the group itself), or some combination of the two. The level of group support and integration necessary to keep individual behavior normative varies inversely with the intensity of the individual's attachment to the norms. The more a person has internalized the norms, the lower the level of group supports required to keep his behavior normative. Conversely, at a specified level of individual attachment to norms, the fewer the group supports available, the smaller the likelihood that behavior will be normative. In our previous examples, the professor requires continuing rewards from his colleagues in order to keep him coming to faculty meetings. As he has few internal pressures to do so, he needs more external support. The businessman, on the other hand, needs less external pressure because his internal pressures are quite strong enough.

It is important to note that a group may regard a person's behavior as normative by its standards, even though the person does not support them. For example, some faculty members will perform administrative duties without really being committed to a norm that calls upon them to do so. But their colleagues will still view their behavior as normative. At the same time, any behavior that is deviant from a group point of view because it violates group norms also involves the absence of, or reduction of, individual commitment to group norms. But, from the individual's point of view, such deviant behavior *may* represent adherence and commitment to the norms of some other social group that he regards as more significant. If the professor fails to perform his administrative duties, for example, he will be judged deviant by at least some of his colleagues. But he may feel that his avoidance of administrative tasks and his preference for research is not deviant, but that it represents his adherence to the norms of his profession, which emphasize research. Behavior that is called deviant by one group (colleagues in his university) may be treated as desirable by another group (colleagues at other universities).

Two important points emerge from this discussion. First, there must be mechanisms of behavior motivation and control in addition to the normative regulation of behavior. Behavior can be deemed normative even in the absence of personal commitment, and it can fail to be normative even where there is personal support for the norms. It is important to specify the nature of such nonnormative determinants of behavior. Second, deviant behavior must be defined in social terms; that is, we must keep in mind that the labeling of behavior as deviant is done by particular social groups in relation to their own norms. We cannot expect to find full consensus on norms in any society, so behavior that is deviant for one group may well be normative for another.

Power

The second mechanism of behavior motivation and control is power, which is the potential held by a person or group to attain some goal. This may involve the need to control or influence the behavior of another person or group. Very frequently when such influence is employed, it rests upon the threat or use of sanctions against a person or group to secure the desired behavior. Power should, however, be distinguished from authority, which is *legitimate* power. Behavior that results from the exercise of authority is *normatively* governed because the individual supports norms that give others the right to exercise power over him. Power involves no such right, at least from the point of view of the person over whom it is exercised. For example, men may be conscripted into military service against their will, poor people may pay excessive rates of interest to loan sharks under the threat of violence, and welfare recipients' lives are to a great extent regulated by a welfare bureaucracy. The distinction between power and authority, however, is not always perfectly clear. Just as members of a particular group may define their behavior as normative by their own standards—even though it is labeled deviant by others—they may also feel that the attempts of others to control or influence their behavior represent the use of coercion, not authority. When speaking of authority, it is always necessary to specify who regards the power it entails as legitimate and who does not. In one sense, loan sharks, the directors of the Selective Service System, and welfare bureaucrats are quite similar: Some or all of their clients do not regard their power as legitimate. On another plane, however, there are real differences. While few members of the society would impute legitimacy to the power of loan sharks over those in debt to them, most members of the society would regard Selective Service officials and welfare officials as exercising authority.

Because some behavior results from the use of power, behavior may be defined as deviant by powerful members of society if it departs from their *coercive* expectations. Such behavior is called "deviant" by those who have the power to coerce but not by the person engaging in it, and it may or may not reflect commitment to social norms in conflict with the coercive expectations. A person may fail to do what those who hold power over him wish him to do because the norms of a group to which he belongs call for violation. For example, Amish parents resist attempts by outsiders (public officials) to make their children attend state-certified schools; their social group values its own traditions above those of the society as a whole. Behavior may also violate coercive expectations of powerful people without at the same time being responsive to social norms. This possibility implies a third mechanism of behavioral motivation and control.

Before we define that third mechanism, a reminder about the definition of deviant behavior is in order. Whether behavior is normative or coerced, it is characterized as deviant by members of society who uphold the relevant norms or coercive expectations. Behavior is deviant when it is so defined. When we speak of deviant behavior we imply nothing more than the simple fact that it violates certain social expectations.

Situational Demands

The third mechanism of behavioral control and motivation is situational demands. Some behavior is determined by a combination of psychological predispositions and external events over which the individual has no control, rather than from normative motivation or coercion. This category of behavior consists mainly of responsive or adaptive behavior; the individual behaves as he does in order to adapt himself to his situation. The soldier, for example, adapts his previous training to the need to survive in a particular combat situation. Here, adaptation refers to physical survival, but it need not. An unemployed and husbandless slum mother, for example, may engage in welfare cheating or in sexual relationships that the society defines as illicit. Her behavior is not the result of normative preferences nor of the efforts of others to exert control over her (no one tries to make her behave as she does in order to secure their goals). Rather, her behavior is an attempt to adjust to her situation by meeting her own physical and psychological needs and those of her children as best she can. In real instances of behavior, of course, responses to the situation frequently blend with behavior that is controlled by norms or coercion. The soldier in combat is responding to the authority of his superiors and to his own sense of duty as well as to the demands for survival in his particular situation. And, the slum mother may be trying to fulfill her duty to her children, even though her behavior would not be widely regarded as normatively acceptable.

Although we cannot sensibly speak of deviation from situational demands, such demands frequently force individuals to violate normative or coercive expectations thus earning them the label "deviant." Theft necessary for physical survival is an example of deviant behavior arising from situational demands. We shall see later that there are instances, especially among delinquent juveniles, in which "psychic survival" is as important as physical survival.

Defining Deviant Behavior

Before defining and classifying any specific instance of behavior as deviant, several other questions must be settled. First, is the behavior governed by norms shared by all members of the society, by the norms of a group of which the individual is a member, by the expectations of powerful groups or individuals, or by no standards at all? Second, does it violate prescriptive or proscriptive norms? Third, does the individual accept norms governing his specific behavior, and has he internalized them? Fourth, are there strong group supports for normative behavior? Fifth, who defines the behavior as deviant—the society as a whole? a powerful group within it? a group to which the person himself belongs? the person himself? Sixth, how seriously is the deviant behavior regarded? Is it treated as a minor deviation or as serious enough to threaten the integrity of the society?

These questions suggest that we must understand both the motivation of the individual and the responses to his behavior of significant social groups. Whether or not any given instance of behavior is defined as deviant depends upon who takes or is assigned responsibility for evaluating it. Explanation of the behavior itself, however, begins with the individual motivation behind it. Of course, we cannot construct a fully satisfactory explanation *only* at that level. If an adolescent boy steals a car, an activity clearly disapproved by the police, we can learn much by asking him about his behavior: how he felt as he committed the offense; why he thinks he did it; how he feels about parents, teachers, policemen, and other adults; how he feels about himself and his chances in life. But if we pay attention only to such information, we shall not discover the structural basis of the social experience and situation out of which his conduct arose. An adequate account of motivation must include its sources in social structure and the situational factors that influence its translation into behavior. To complete our analysis of behavior we must consider social responses to it.

So far we have referred mainly to specific occurrences of behavior that may be classified as deviant or conforming. Often, however, it is more revealing to focus upon constellations of individual behavior, for people do not lead their lives or organize their selves mainly in terms of discrete acts or expectations; rather, conforming and deviant behavior become part of organized roles that people play. We can ask the same questions about the patterning of individual lives in roles that we have asked about discrete acts: Is the behavior pattern part of a widely recognized social role, one recognized by a specific and perhaps even deviant group of which the individual is a member, one recognized only by certain powerful members of the society, or no role at all? Does it violate prescriptive or proscriptive norms? Does the person view his behavior as a legitimate part of his role performance? Are there group supports that reinforce role behavior? Who defines behavior as meeting or not meeting role requirements? How seriously does society view departures from expected role performances?

To contrast the two kinds of questions, we could examine an instance of theft as an isolated and disconnected crime and could ask questions like the following: Is theft widely condemned by the members of society? Is it condemned or supported by groups of which the thief is a member? Does the thief support legal norms that prohibit stealing other people's property, or does he support norms that justify theft? Do the social groups of which the thief is a member provide rewards for keeping within the law or for violating it? Does the person regard his theft as a deviant act and himself as a deviant person? We may also ask slightly different but corresponding questions: Is this theft one instance of a pattern of illegal behavior by the thief? Do other members of his social groups share this pattern? Does theft fulfill a role obligation in the view of the thief and the groups to which he belongs? Does any group provide information, technique, and a system of rewards for such behavior? Is theft part of the person's definition of his own social role and his social identity? Questions at this level reflect the tendency to organize behavior in terms of clusters of norms, coercive expectations, and situational demands.

Behavior that is socially defined as deviant is clearly not a simple phenomenon subject to a single explanation. Rather, it is complex in its motivation and in its social definition. Particular examples of behavior that are socially defined as deviant (because they violate the normative or coercive expectations of others) may result from many different motivations; any particular motivation may lead to various forms of behavior, some of which may be called "deviant" and some "conforming." For example, the kind of deviant behavior called "crimes against property" probably results from several different motives; some men steal or destroy property to express their outrage at the alleged immorality of others, some do it for fun, others seek to enhance their own material position (perhaps out of necessity), and still others are guided by psychological dispositions beyond voluntary control. A single motive, like the desire for more success symbols than can be acquired through legitimate channels may lead to different forms of behavior: Some people attempt to acquire the symbols illicitly; others find life unbearable without them and turn to suicide; and others take refuge in mental illness. Whether defined as deviant or conforming, behavior is always a product of the motivations and capabilities of individuals and of the situations in which they find themselves. The same motivations and capabilities will produce different behavior in different situations, and similar situations will call forth different behavior, according to various individual motivations and capabilities.

Social Stratification

Social stratification is the hierarchical ordering of the members of a society into strata according to several criteria of rank. The criteria most commonly used by members of a society to rank one another are power, property, and prestige.[4] A stratum consists of a large number of people who share a common or similar rank with respect to one or more of these and other criteria. Men command unequal shares of the goods and services available in almost every society and unequal power to influence their own and others' lives. In every society they are ranked on one or more scales of value: social worth or productivity, ritual purity, conformity to moral codes, the difficulty of the work they do, to name but a few. Such inequalities are *socially structured* because they do not result mainly from individual differences in effort, initiative, or ability—although these differences nearly always play some part—but are built into society. To state that the inequalities are socially structured is to imply that they are not accidental, but institutionalized—that they are somehow related to the important values of the society. There is also an implication that inequalities are transmitted from one generation to the next:

The wealth, power, and prestige of parents help to ensure comparable levels for their children. And there is usually some implication that these three types of inequality, along with others, are correlated to some extent—that the wealthy are also the powerful and command the most prestige.

The main emphasis in this book is upon *prestige*, which involves *differential evaluation*. Our later discussion of inequality in relation to self-esteem and deviant behavior will emphasize inequalities of prestige. Every thing, event, person, and position in a society is ranked on value scales. People, the positions they occupy, their personal and social characteristics, and the goods and services they command are evaluated in degrees of desirability, morality, worthiness of respect, ritual purity, pleasantness, competence, goodness.[5] This continuing process is called "differential evaluation." Prestige is a characteristic of individuals, and it results from differential evaluation in a variety of concrete *contexts of interaction*. A context of interaction is simply a place and a time in which interaction among people takes place.

Stratification by prestige occurs when members of a society are ranked according to social evaluations of their positions, possessions, performances, and attributes. *Positions* are places in the network of social relationships; of all the positions available, some are evaluated and ranked in terms of prestige. For example, a society might evaluate only the occupational positions but make no evaluative distinctions between age and sex categories. *Possessions* are goods and services acquired by individuals, including various forms of property. *Performances* are forms of behavior that are not associated with specific positions or that are outside the minimum standards of behavior associated with specific social positions. Heroism "beyond the call of duty" would be included in this category, as would exceptional success as a father or as a businessman. *Attributes* are personal qualities that are either unique to the individual or that reflect social position, such as strength, interpersonal capabilities, and such ascribed characteristics as race, ethnic affiliation, religion, and family lineage.

In summary, members of a society can be ranked on the basis of a number of criteria. In this analysis, we are concerned mainly with stratification by prestige, since we shall later attempt to relate individuals' prestige evaluations to their self-evaluations and their resulting propensities for various forms of behavior. A society may contain a small number of very precisely defined prestige strata (as in a caste system), or it may be much more ambigously stratified, with only vague dividing lines on which there is not much agreement between the major strata. Individuals acquire prestige rank on the basis of the evaluations—which rest upon a large number of positions, possessions, performances, and attributes—they receive from others. The prestige a person acquires, therefore, depends partly upon his social position—his occupation, for example—and partly upon other factors—his success in acquiring material goods, his ability to perform exceptionally well in various positions, or his membership in religious or ethnic groups. Since these evaluations are received in many different contexts, the person builds up a self-image of his own prestige, as well as a public reputation, over an extended period of time.

Total Consensus on Ranking

We can begin to describe how societies become stratified by prestige by suggesting the limits within which the process operates and by outlining some social factors that keep them well within those limits. It is possible to imagine a society in which the position of each individual on a prestige scale could be exactly and completely known by every other individual. Each combination of social positions, possessions, performances, and attributes would yield a "prestige score" that could be compared with all other such scores. Mr. Jones could add up his full professorship, his position as husband and father, his comfortable home and fine car, his professional talents, his service to the local Boy Scouts, and his renowned family name and WASP background; he could then compare the resulting score with that of someone else.

It is in fact difficult for any society to maintain so complete and precise a system of ranking, which depends upon widespread knowledge of evaluative criteria (how to rank various combinations of positions, possessions, performances, and attributes) and upon equally widespread mutual acquaintance so that all necessary information on every individual would be available. These conditions are impossible in all but the simplest societies with small populations.

As societies become more complex—creating new positions and roles, new institutions, and more diverse groups with only partially overlapping memberships—it becomes more difficult to disseminate all the necessary information and to secure agreement on the criteria of evaluation themselves. Statements about the relative value of positions, performances, possessions, and attributes have implications about the worth of the men who have them. Although men *may* be motivated to accept and support value systems in which they receive low ratings, there is no reason to believe that such acceptance can be accomplished easily and as a matter of course.[6] Men accept definitions of themselves as socially, morally, or otherwise inferior only with difficulty; consequently, societies are able to generate consensus on the criteria of evaluation only with difficulty and frequently not at all. Furthermore, a complete ranking system would require a refined social calculus in which positions, possessions, performances, and attributes could be measured in terms of one common denominator and combined in single total scores. Professor Jones might have little difficulty evaluating himself, but in comparing himself with others things would become sticky. How would his full professorship and moderate wealth be compared to another's associate professorship and inherited fortune? What points are to be assigned to each attribute, and how are they to be added? Even if there were consensus on the criteria of evaluation—and even if they were few enough to be manageable—the system could not work unless all members of the society participated in a common network of social relationships, enabling them to assemble the information necessary to make differential evaluations. But, again such networks are likely to exist only in small premodern societies.

Total Equality

At the opposite extreme from total consensus on ranking would be the complete absence of inequality, or at least a condition in which none of the existing inequalities would be regarded as significant enough to justify differential evaluation. There is no society in which there are *no* inequalities, and inequalities invariably result in at least some differential evaluation and prestige ranking. Is the unequal allocation of prestige (or of anything else) functionally necessary for the survival of a society? Kingsley Davis and Wilbert Moore have argued that inequalities in rewards and evaluations are necessary in order to match positions of unequal difficulty and importance with men of appropriate talents.[7] The ubiquity of inequality can be construed as evidence of such necessity, but this ubiquity may also be construed as evidence of man's failure so far to invent alternatives to inequality in the performance of the functions that inequality performs. We cannot say that inequality is inevitable, as we obviously do not yet have evidence on societies of the future. It is more useful, therefore, to avoid considering what *must be* and to deal instead with what *is*: Differential evaluation and the ranking of individuals in terms of prestige are universal, and the results always fall between conditions of complete inequality and complete equality.

Power and Prestige-Bargaining

In this book we treat the individual as the focus of differential evaluation, and in doing so we depart from the conventional emphasis upon *positions* as the focus of this process. Although it is true that positions are themselves subject to prestige ranking— and it is important to explain just why they are ranked in a given way—our concern is with the impact of differential evaluation upon individuals themselves.

Differential evaluation and the assignment of prestige do not, of course, take place in a social vacuum: A person does not "read" his prestige from a set of ideal specifications. Instead he finds them in clubs and in churches, on the streets and in homes, and wherever people meet and assess one another. Each participant in any context of social interaction evaluates others by the criteria that he believes important. There is no evidence that the survival of society requires all members of a society, or even all participants in a single context of interaction, to support the same criteria of evaluation. Indeed, in a complex society it is probable that the criteria of evaluation will be diverse and that they will be differentially supported by its members. For this reason we speak of *ideologies of prestige*, sets of ideal beliefs that define the scope and nature of differential evaluation and justify specific criteria of evaluation.

Ideologies of prestige take various forms. They may be global, as the Protestant Ethic is, or much more limited in scope, as the current slogan of the Black Revolution, "Black is Beautiful." The former, for example, functions not only as a driving force behind individual effort and accomplishment but is also a framework of beliefs and values that allows the individual to feel satisfaction and pride in his own accomplishments and to evaluate others and their work. The latter is an attempt to redefine a specific traditional criterion of evaluation in American society, which has identified "black" with ugliness and evil, in an effort to create new bases for blacks to take pride in themselves. Ideologies of prestige may also be found in widely shared beliefs that are deeply imbedded in the fabric of a culture, such as the belief, which is prevalent in industrial societies, that manual work is inferior in value to nonmanual work—that it is better to work with the brain than with the hands. It is important to keep in mind that ideologies of prestige consist of all kinds of beliefs and values that affect the evaluative process, and not just those that are popularly associated with "social class."

Ideologies of prestige are intimately linked with the social distribution of power in three important ways. First, relative power may be a criterion of evaluation in any ideology of prestige. As an attribute of position, power may help to shape evaluation of the position, either favorably or unfavorably. In industrial societies occupations that confer large amounts of power (corporation executive, Federal politician, physician) are usually ranked higher than occupations that do not (manual laborer, salesman, clerk). Second, power has considerable influence on the process of evaluation in an actual context of interaction. In a factory, for example, managers have authority over workers that may extend to social interaction in which prestige evaluations are made. The manager may expect (and workers may have to yield) deference that is not justified by the functional requirements of the job. Inequalities of power may also result from differences in age, sex, talents, and social competence. Such inequalities of power are important because of the nature of the bargaining process that takes place within contexts of interaction. Some participants in a context claim prestige from others, and the ability to do so and to have their claims accepted may depend upon their power relative to that of others. While factory workers who defer to a manager may in reality hold him in contempt, their deference constitutes a form of reinforcement for his own self-image of prestige as well as for the workers' understanding of what the society values.

Third, power is important in determining the visibility of ideologies of prestige. The power to promote and publicize an ideology of prestige rests upon control over means of promotion and publicity. In a modern society these means include the media of mass communication, as well as many social agencies for the dissemination of knowledge and beliefs: for example, schools, religious organizations, political parties, places of employment. The ideologies of prestige created and promoted through these agencies constitute enduring and visible bases for determining any individual's prestige ranking, reinforcing adherence to those ideologies and challenging the disaffected. Such visible ideologies contribute heavily to the impression of order and consensus in the system of prestige allocation, particularly in a modern society. Of course, consensus on ideologies of prestige is not entirely illusory, as many people do support dominant ideologies even though they do not fare well by them, many others assent by default, failing to formulate counter ideologies.

Nevertheless in a modern society there are likely to be many competing ideologies of prestige. Under such conditions, individuals support those that guarantee to them the highest rankings possible.[8] For example, the wealthy man will probably believe that possessions are the most significant mark of a man's worth, and the well-educated will argue for the priority of education in assigning prestige. Those who are able to claim prestige on the basis of no scarce criteria—positions, possessions, performances, and attributes that grant high prestige are either naturally scarce, or the society contrives to make them scarce

—will claim it on the basis of more widely applicable criteria like moral behavior, exceptional role performance within the family, and the like.

Within contexts of interaction, people make known their own claims to relative ranking and their responses to the claims of others. This process is called *prestige-bargaining*, in which each person seeks to gain the highest prestige possible in return for the least expenditure of recognition for the claims of others. The more impersonal and autonomous the context of interaction, the more prestige claims and the bargaining process depend upon visible symbols,[9] usually in the form of possessions. When a bargain is struck, it may involve powerful coalitions of participants who set the tone of the prestige process and define and reserve the highest ranks for themselves, it may involve genuine consensus on the criteria of evaluation, or it may involve mutual agreement on equal treatment of all. But a bargain may not be struck at all, and then continuing negotiations may color all subsequent social action within the context.

Within the modern corporation, for example, those who hold power and authority generally also define the evaluating criteria *within* the organization. They tend to define success in promoting the goals of the organization as the main criteria of evaluation (although criteria unrelated to achievement, such as friendships or family backgrounds, may enter the picture) and to reserve the highest evaluations for themselves, commanding deference, if not respect, from lower ranks. For members of the organization who are not highly evaluated within it, the organization comes to be regarded negatively—and as insignificant to their own sense of worth, although their negative work experiences may well injure their sense of worth—and they turn elsewhere for more favorable evaluations.

The small-scale, primitive society is quite often characterized by a different type of prestige-bargaining process. In a setting where men are continuously engaged in a quest for food and shelter, for example, a man's achievements in the hunt may well be the only basis for differential evaluation. In this case, there will probably be a high degree of consensus among the members of the group about the validity of this criterion and the relative standing of everyone in terms of it.

In other settings, strong egalitarian ideologies may reduce prestige-bargaining to a minimum. In sports, for example, it is frequently considered bad form to boast of one's ability or accomplishments; the team is considered by its members to be the important unit, not the individual. When the prohibition against special individual recognition is violated, strong sanctions are frequently applied. In effect, the team has been declared off-limits to prestige-bargaining.

The outcome of prestige-bargaining in any given context depends upon numerous factors. Sometimes bargains are enforced by powerful participants, and when they are, those who receive the lowest evaluations may grant prestige contemptuously and withdraw from interaction in that context. Often, the participants recognize that prestige-bargaining would be disruptive to their activities, so they declare it off-limits. But, where consensus on ideologies of prestige is high, such as in a primitive community, there is also likely to be consensus on prestige ranks and little prestige-bargaining. Conversely, where there is much lack of consensus, where no group can effectively dominate, and where participants see no compelling reason to refrain from prestige-bargaining, then action may be dominated by prestige negotiations.

The modern middle-class practice of "keeping up with the Joneses" provides an example of continuous prestige-bargaining. Often in middle-class society, there is great competition for prestige through acquisitions and other displays of affluence, such as vacations to far-off lands. Yet, prestige-bargaining can have positive benefits. For example, a member of a profession who desires to acquire professional recognition for his work may derive much of his drive for professional accomplishment from that drive.

Prestige ranking is thus an immediate process in which we all participate continually. We interact with others in stores, in factories, in classrooms, in libraries, on the street, and myriad other places. We constantly make claims for our own prestige—by assuming command, by showing deference or by showing that we expect deference, by habits of speech and gesture, and by what we say. We are also constantly exposed to the similar claims of others; sometimes we submit to their claims, and sometimes they yield to ours. An individual's image of his own relative prestige depends upon his cumulative experience in prestige-bargaining with others.

In matters of prestige allocation, as in any social arrangement, there are likely to be disparities between the expectations of the participants and what actually occurs. We must distinguish between the ideal process of differential evaluation implied by an ideology of prestige and the actual allocation of prestige that results from bargaining. The disparities are closely related to the sociological distinction between ascription and achievement.

Some ideologies of prestige emphasize ascriptive criteria as the sole basis for prestige ranking. In a pure caste system, for example, membership through birth in a legally and religiously defined caste group exclusively and unalterably determines social prestige. No matter how strongly the ideology is asserted, however, there is always some social mobility within the system. If not individuals then at least subcastes are able to improve their positions on one or more scales of ranking over a span of years.[10] Therefore some element of achievement enters the system, and correlations among position (caste), income, occupation, and other attributes are imperfect. Even the most logically integrated ideology never corresponds precisely to the actual operation of society, simply because every social system generates strains and tensions that require it from time to time to subordinate its ideologies to other demands.

There are also systems of social stratification in which major emphasis is placed upon individual achievement, rather than upon inherited position. Social rewards are presumably accessible to all on the basis of individual performance and merit. But the actual always departs from the ideal, frequently to a large degree, because ascriptive elements corrupt emphasis upon achievement. Children, for example, are almost universally accorded prestige along with their parents. Similarly, ethnic affiliation is a powerful determinant of prestige and frequently tends to supersede achievement as a criterion of evaluation. Actual behavior thus very often departs significantly from official belief in equality of opportunity to achieve.

One implication of this discussion of prestige is that a person's prestige is not necessarily a stable personal attribute but may vary from one social context to another. His cumulative experiences in prestige-bargaining situations include elements that tend toward inconsistency and instability, as well as elements that promote consistency and stability; it is important to examine how these elements balance each other. The member of a small community in which his personal or family visibility is high—and that offers a stable network of interpersonal relationships and contexts of interaction encompassing most of the community—is more likely to receive a consistent picture of his own prestige rank. Individuals in such a community have fixed prestige, in the sense that they are likely to be exposed to a fairly constant set of contexts of social interaction and thus to a fairly constant set of evaluations of themselves. Of course, they may not *agree* that their socially awarded ranks are just. Furthermore, a stable set of evaluations in different contexts of interaction *need not* be consistent. A person may shop regularly in the same stores, go to work, encounter the same public officials, entertain the same circle of friends, yet receive within each context a different image of his prestige in the community. Even so, he may achieve some sense of consistency by paying more attention to some evaluations than to others. As communities grow in size the number of available interaction contexts increases, and there are more ways in which criteria of evaluation can be elaborated and inconsistent rankings produced. At the same time, however, the choice of associations within such communities partly reduces the inconsistency of evaluations that an individual receives: Social interaction is carried on most frequently and intensively among those who consider themselves equals.

Two considerations nevertheless make it likely that many individuals in more complex communities will receive inconsistent images of their own prestige. First, mass media and other public channels of communication continue to publicize certain prestige ideologies. Second, people cannot always avoid relationships that require them to accord higher status to others. For example, the unemployed manual worker hears frequent public assertions that individuals are morally responsible for their own conditions; furthermore he must often turn for help to middle-class officials, and part of the price for their assistance may be his own abasement. The effects of such experiences cannot be wholly overcome by more positive evaluations from his friends and family.

Prestige, then, is not to be considered as a fixed attribute of each member of a society; rather it is a shifting property in the determination of which each member of a society participates. In specific places and at specific times when people interact with one another, individuals devote attention and energy to the question of how good, how well off, how deserving, how worthy each particpant is relative to the others. How much time and energy, and with what results, depends upon the specific participants and their characteristics, the extent of agreement on appropriate criteria of prestige allocation, and who has how much power within the context.

Stratification in American Society

We turn now to stratification in American society. We shall discuss several important propositions that will provide the basis for a more detailed analysis of stratification and its consequences for deviant behavior in subsequent chapters.

The dominant criteria of differential evaluation in American society are occupation, income, and education. A feature of industrial society is that occupations are the social positions most important for differential evaluation, perhaps because the work that men do intimately affects their life chances and life styles. Even though prestige ideologies often stress the intrinsic worth of all men, occupational status is the single most important basis for according prestige, honor, and respect. The impressive similarities among occupational prestige rankings within several industrial societies and the relative stability of such rankings in American society suggest widespread acceptance of occupation as a criterion of evaluation in industrial societies.[11]

In American society, income is an important determinant of the prestige accorded an occupation. It is also a major independent criterion of evaluation. There are few serious external restrictions on use of income, and men can adopt whatever life styles and consumption practices they can afford; these styles and practices often signal the prestige that they believe is due them. Because income level is only imperfectly associated with occupational prestige, some men find it possible to purchase the symbols of higher prestige levels than would be accorded them solely on the basis of their occupations. Still others cannot afford the symbols of the prestige that they believe is due them because, though their occupations help them to earn high prestige, they receive relatively low incomes.

Education as a criterion of evaluation is to some degree independent of occupation and income. It is a highly valued personal attribute in industrial societies and can enter significantly into prestige bargaining, sometimes as reinforcement of prestige claims entered on other grounds and sometimes as a substitute for occupational or income prestige. For example, poorly paid public-school teachers may claim prestige on grounds of educational attainment, and even self-educated prison inmates may claim respect for their accomplishments.

The dominant American ideology of prestige stresses achievement at the expense of ascription. Evaluation is ideally based on occupation, income, and education attained through effort rather than birth. Upward social mobility is regarded as a prime virtue, and everyone is regarded as eligible to compete for success. In the dominant ideology of prestige, the most admired are those who most successfully pursue the "American dream" of success, which is presumably accessible to all. As Robert K. Merton has suggested, the ideology regards failure as shameful only when it is accompanied by loss of ambition.[12] Social mobility is itself regarded as evidence of a man's worth and as an indicator of the prestige that he deserves.

Whether highest prestige should be accorded to those who travel the greatest distance upward in the social scale or to those who achieve the highest absolute level is ambiguous in American ideology. It simultaneously asserts the value of effort and of attainment, which can lead to inconsistencies, but it is not unusual for an ideology to lack perfect internal consistency. In fact Americans are more frequently rated for what they *have* and *are* than for the *effort* they have expended.

The American achievement-oriented ideology is modified in

operation by several ascriptive elements. Several social criteria that run counter to the dominant ideology of achievement have an important impact upon differential evaluation. We can clearly identify four such criteria. First, evaluations based on skin color, ethnic origins, and religious beliefs frequently counteract those that would be made on grounds of income, occupation, and education. For example, many Americans would evaluate a black physician according to their low opinion of his race rather than according to their high opinion of his occupation. Such criteria, though subversive of the dominant ideology, have shown remarkable tenacity, but they are less important today than they once were.

Second, many of the main symbols of prestige in American society can be purchased. But, although consumption is a convenient clue to income and position, it does not reflect the effort expended and the obstacles overcome to attain them. The main emphasis is upon having them, and distinctions between those who have inherited them and those who have achieved them by merit and effort are weakened.

Third, children participate in interaction contexts, schools for example, in which they are evaluated according to the social strata of their parents. Society does not suspend judgment until the evidence of the son's adult performance is in, but evaluates him in advance, according to the position and attainments of his father.

Fourth, although the American ideology of prestige emphasizes that failure need be only temporary for those who seek to better themselves, nevertheless those who are paid the least, who are employed in the most menial and least steady occupations, and who receive the least and poorest education often take a fatalistic view. They see themselves as trapped in a cruel, unyielding system.

We have presented here only the outlines of stratification in American society, with particular attention to the allocation of prestige. In later chapters we shall fill in these outlines and explore the impact of social arrangements on behavior. The immediate task is the construction of a theoretical link between social stratification, as we have described it, and deviant behavior.

Notes

1. A good explanation of "deductive nomological explanation," as well as a useful analysis of functionalism in sociology, can be found in Carl G. Hempel, "The Logic of Functional Analysis," in Llewellyn Gross, ed., *Symposium on Sociological Theory* (New York: Harper, 1959), 271–307.
2. Our use of the word "commitment" follows that of Wilbert Moore and Arnold Feldman in *Labor Commitment and Social Change in Developing Areas* (New York: Social Science Research Council, 1960), especially the chapter on social stratification, "Competing Status Systems," by Melvin M. Tumin, 277–290.
3. *Cf.* David Riesman, Reuel Denney, and Nathan Glazer, *The Loney Crowd* (New Haven: Yale University Press, 1950); and Margaret Mead, *And Keep Your Powder Dry* (New York: Morrow, 1942).
4. More extended treatments of social stratification can be found in Kurt Mayer, *Class and Society* (rev. ed., New York: Random House, 1955); and Melvin M. Tumin, *Social Stratification: The Forms and Functions of Inequality* (Englewood Cliffs, N.J.: Prentice-Hall, 1967). For a detailed treatment see Gerhard Lenski, *Power and Privilege* (New York: McGraw-Hill, 1966).
5. This use of "differential evaluation" is similar to that of Talcott Parsons in "A Revised Analytical Approach to the Theory of Social Stratification," in Parsons, *Essays in Sociological Theory* (New York: Free Press, 1954), 386–439.
6. For an outstanding discussion of this problem see Erving Goffman, *Stigma: Notes on the Management of Spoiled Identity* (Englewood Cliffs, N.J.: Prentice-Hall, 1963).
7. The controversy over the functions of social inequality is an interesting and important one. Students should begin with Kingsley Davis and Moore, "Some Principles of Stratification," *American Sociological Review, 10* (1945), 242–249; and Tumin, "Some Principles of Stratification: A Critical Analysis," *American Sociological Review, 18* (1953), 387–394.
8. Students should attempt, as an exercise, to discover the assumptions about human behavior and its motivation that underlie this proposition.
9. See William H. Form and G. P. Stone, "Urbanism, Anonymity, and Status Symbolism," *American Journal of Sociology, 62* (1957), 504–514.
10. Under such circumstances there is group rather than individual mobility. Individuals remain part of their caste, or subcaste, but the group as a whole improves its position relative to other such groups.

11. See National Opinion Research Center, "Jobs and Occupations: A Popular Evaluation," *Opinion News* (September 1, 1947), 3–13; and Alex Inkeles and Peter Rossi, "National Camparisons of Occupational Prestige," *American Journal of Sociology, 61* (1956), 329–339.
12. See Robert K. Merton, *Social Theory and Social Structure* (rev. ed., New York: Free Press, 1957), Chapter 4.

Self-Esteem
and
the Regulation
of
Behavior

2

In this chapter we shall develop a set of social-psychological propositions that will enable us to link social inequality and deviant behavior. In doing so we shall take the position that a person's concept of himself plays a central role in his behavior.

Sociologists frequently forget that social structures represent the patterned and repetitive actions of individuals; psychologists as frequently neglect to consider that individual characteristics are developed largely under the influence of social structure. The concept of the *self* can bridge this gap between sociologism and psychologism. One of the distinctive characteristics of human organisms is that they have *selves*—that they are neither perfectly socialized automatons absolutely molded by society nor completely autonomous individuals responsive only to personal needs and impulses. Social behavior is oriented toward the self —an entity partly shaped by social experiences comes to play an independent role in shaping and responding to future experiences.

One of the most fruitful sources of theory about the self is the social-psychological tradition developed by George Herbert Mead and the symbolic interactionists.[1] They distinguish the self from the physiological organism by the fact that it develops in the course of socialization. In early socialization the individual experiences himself indirectly "from the particular standpoints of other individual members of the same social group or from the generalized standpoint of the social group as a whole to which he belongs."[2] He is shaped to significant degrees by seeing himself as others see him. In forming a concept of himself he takes into account the reactions of others to his behavior, their feelings and attitudes, approval or disapproval.

But what *is* the self? Although there are many different ways of conceptualizing the self, one useful way is to divide the self into five major components. The first component is an organized set of motivations. The person's behavior is not characterized by randomness, but is marked by a tendency to pursue certain goals (such as the satisfaction of basic drives like sex or hunger, the approval of other people, or material possessions) and to avoid conditions that are unpleasant or painful. These motivations are organized in relation to each other, as well as to other aspects of the self. For example, basic drives, such as hunger and sex, take precedence over such learned motives as prestige or possessions. And, some of a person's motivations relate to his commitments to social norms or his repertory of roles, both of which are also components of the self. The second component of the self, in fact, is a series of social roles to which the person is committed, along with a knowledge of how to play them. Social roles are clusters of norms that are related to particular positions that the person occupies. Each position—father, student, professor—has an associated role and, as the self develops, a set of commitments to those roles is incorporated within it. Here, there is a clear implication that part of what a person is consists of what he does and what he believes he should do in the performance of his roles. The third component of the self is a more general set of commitments to social norms and their underlying values. Sometimes these norms are internalized and sometimes they are not. Many norms are not tied to particular roles, but instead constitute standards of behavior that may be widely shared. These norms are often quite general in scope (for example, the belief that men should be treated equally or that the elderly should be treated with respect) and, like roles, help to define what a person is. The fourth component of the self is a set of cognitive abilities, including the ability to create and understand symbols, which guide response to the intended meanings of others in social interaction and provide a "map" of the physical and social setting in which the person finds himself. Such abilities, which exist as a potential in the infant and are powerfully shaped during socialization, are requisite to the development of organized motives and commitments to norms and roles. The fifth and final component of the self is a set of ideas about one's qualities, capabilities, commitments, and motives—a self-image—that is developed by the individual in the course of his socialization. The self, then, may be defined as a set of potentials and predispositions for behavior that are organized in terms of these components.

This analysis of the self suggests some of the qualities that people develop as they evolve from infancy into adequately functioning adult members of society. This evolutionary process is called *socialization*. People develop more or less organized sets of motivations—that is, they develop certain persistent wants and needs, seek satisfactions of particular kinds, pursue individual goals, and come to prefer some rewards to others. They become committed to sets of social roles—that is, they develop the skills and techniques necessary to behave as fathers, physicians, citizens, and so on. They develop commitments to social norms, learning to behave as society expects (that is, as their parents, families, and other groups of people who are important to them expect) and to believe that it is right to do so. They develop a large number of cognitive skills, learning to perceive the world in which they live much as others perceive it and to discern the motives and interests of others. Finally, they develop *self-images*; that is, they come to have fairly clear images of the kinds of people they are and think they ought to be.

In this book we shall pay special attention to the self-image and the way in which it evolves. During socialization, there is mutual interdependence between the self-image, on one hand, and motivations, roles, normative commitments, and cognitive skills, on the other. Morris Rosenberg has argued that the self-image can be analyzed in terms of the dimensions common to all attitudes: content, direction, intensity, importance, salience, consistency, stability, and clarity.[3] What does the person believe he is? Does he like or dislike what he sees in himself? How much does he like or dislike what he sees? How important is his self in comparison to other objects in his experience? How often does the person think of himself? Are the various parts of his self-image consistent? Does it tend to remain constant or to change from day to day? How clearly defined and perceived is the self?

As we examine the self-image and its formation and try to discover its influence on the individual's motivations, normative commitments, roles and role skills, and cognitive skills—in short, his behavior—we shall find it very useful to pay special attention to three of these dimensions: content, direction, and stability. That is, our attention will be directed to the formation of *self-esteem* and its impact upon behavior. Self-esteem can be usefully defined as a person's feeling that he is what he ought to be, that he is a socially acceptable and worthy person who need make no apology for what he is.

Formation and Behavioral Import of Self-Esteem

The self develops during the course of the person's experience, which is to a great degree shaped by the social arrangements in which he participates: the interpersonal relationships they provide, the statuses and roles they permit him and others, and the standards of evaluation they set forth. It should not be assumed, however, that the self is determined rigidly by social structure. Individuals occupy unique positions in the social structure—because of differences in their families, the resources that they command, their own inherited abilities, the opportunities that are available to them, chance, and similar factors—and thus have somewhat unique experiences. Moreover, as socialization proceeds, the individual tends to become more autonomous—to reflect on his experiences and to attribute meaning to them—and thereafter tends to become even more unique. The behavior patterns that characterize the self depend heavily upon the way in which the person develops and maintains self-esteem. Our task is to show how self-esteem is developed and to trace its influence upon behavior.

All men are normally motivated to develop and maintain adequate self-esteem[4] (the precise meaning of "adequate" will be considered later). This generalization has both psychological and sociological implications, for the behavioral consequences of the desire for self-esteem depend upon individual approaches to, or strategies for, strengthening and managing it.

In evaluating themselves, people rely heavily upon the appraisals of *significant others*.[5] These are people whose evaluations are very important to an individual because he is deeply and emotionally committed to them. Often, as in the case of parents, significant others are those who have provided the individual with his basic vocabulary, his outlook toward the world, and his information about social roles. Parents are significant others because of the very early and intimate contacts established with them, but as the individual grows older he has more freedom in choosing significant others.

One approach to the selection of partners in social interaction is to choose only those who will reinforce the individual's self-esteem. Those who will offer negative appraisals are thus avoided, and their appraisals treated as insignificant. As Hans Gerth and C. Wright Mills have pointed out, the selection of significant others is a continuing process. The "cumulative selection of those persons who are significant for the self is thus in the direction of confirming persons, and the more [the individual] succeeds in limiting his significant others to those who thus confirm his prized self-image, the more strongly he will seek such persons as significant in the future."[6]

But the classification of others as significant does not depend solely upon the kinds of evaluations they provide. If a person could dismiss as insignificant any negative appraisal of himself, self-esteem would hardly be a problem for anyone. Unfortunately, men are not completely free to ignore the negative appraisals of others, and consequently self-esteem can thus be damaged. As Gerth and Mills point out, "the selection of significant others is limited by the institutional position of the person and by the course of his career from one institutional position to another."[7] For example, the child is not entirely free to reject his teachers or to leave class if they evaluate him negatively.

There is no theoretical limitation on the number of significant others that a person can select in the course of his life; the circle of such others may be large or small. The child may derive self-esteem from interaction with parents, relatives, schoolteachers, and other adults outside the family, as well as from his peers. But sometimes he is compelled to withdraw into a tight, protective social circle in which only a few people provide intimate mutual support.

The selection of confirming significant others does not exhaust the possible approaches to the management of self-esteem. Especially during childhood, the individual is accustomed to altering his own behavior in order to earn the esteem of others who are already significant. Children strive for the approval of their parents by attempting to match their behavior to the standards that they believe their parents are trying to set.

If a person cannot or will not adjust his behavior to the expectations of significant others, there is still a further possible strategy for the management of self-esteem, but it is so costly that it may justly be called a "strategy of last resort." He can turn inward and seek self-esteem in fantastic self-evaluations. Such a retreat into fantasy is an occasional crutch for many people, used to see them through infrequent negative appraisals. Both children and adults frequently imagine how good and worthy they are when significant others have told them that they are not. But for some people retreating into fantasy becomes a persistent adaptation to a social world that is predominantly threatening and demeaning.

Self-evaluations, however, do not consist entirely of fantasy. As the self develops in the course of socialization, the person tends to become increasingly autonomous, both in the control of his own behavior and in his self-esteem and self-image. This autonomy involves a growing ability to employ standards of behavior in evaluating oneself and an increasing stability of self-image and self-esteem, which allow most people to become increasingly less dependent upon others' appraisals. Thus, as the person gets older, his self-esteem is less vulnerable to the negative appraisals of others, and he also may be less susceptible to improvements stemming from positive appraisals. Paradoxically, those who reach adulthood with low self-esteem may be motivated to secure the approval of others and build self-esteem, while finding it difficult to accept positive responses from others as relevant to self-esteem.

We argue, then, that people are motivated to hold themselves in high esteem and that they have three techniques for doing so: matching their behavior to the standards of significant others who reward them with favorable evaluations; selecting as significant others those who reinforce self-esteem; or retreating from social intercourse into fantasy when efforts are blocked.

The growth of self-esteem is related to the development of commitments to social norms. Melvin M. Tumin has argued that "men will follow that course of behavior designed to enhance their own favorable conceptions of themselves to the maximum available. . . . Morality is maintained to the extent that ego is enhanced by moral behavior and the reception given it."[8] A person's commitment to social norms is partly contingent upon his ability to derive reinforcement for his self-esteem from it.

We have defined commitment as behavior in accord with norms combined with acceptance of their validity. If a person's behavior earns him the esteem of significant others, he becomes more committed to the norms underlying that behavior: Both the desire to repeat the behavior in the future and belief in the rightness of it are enhanced. On the other hand, if behavior that a person believes to be proper does not earn him esteem, his commitment will be diminished.

People with low self-esteem have difficulty in sustaining rewarding interpersonal relationships. According to Harry Stack Sullivan, a person who displays "customarily low self-esteem" is handicapped in his ability to "find himself comfortably able to manifest good feeling toward another person."[9] People who do not think well of themselves have trouble thinking well of others and thus find it difficult to get along with them.

The connection between low self-esteem and difficulties in interpersonal relationships is confirmed by existing evidence.

Rosenberg's data show that adolescents with low self-esteem are more likely to be awkward with others, to be shy, and to have difficulty initiating conversations even with people they know; they are less likely to regard themselves as easy to get along with, to adjust to different kinds of people, and to trust other people.[10]

There is also evidence that self-esteem is associated with anxiety. According to Rosenberg, adolescents with unstable self-images and low self-esteem exhibit more psychosomatic symptoms than do other adolescents, and those with low self-esteem are more sensitive to criticism than are those with high self-esteem. The same findings are reported by Rosenberg in relation to a group of young adults for whom the special problems of self-esteem that may characterize adolescents have presumably diminished.[11]

This link with anxiety is useful in determining when self-esteem can be called "adequate." We say that self-esteem is adequate when the individual feels secure enough to interact successfully with others. As self-esteem improves, anxiety is reduced, and the individual is better able to carry on social relationships. That is, as the person feels better disposed toward others, he is able to feel comfortable enough with them to participate in the normal give-and-take of social interaction, and he is less vulnerable to others' criticism. That people attempt to keep self-esteem at adequate levels means that they strive to strengthen it to the point at which anxieties about self are reduced to tolerable levels. The level at which self-esteem becomes adequate is not the same for everyone, however, as some people are able to tolerate higher levels of anxiety than are others.

We have stated three propositions to specify the behavioral consequences of self-esteem. The first asserts that motivation for maintaining self-esteem at a level adequate to prevent the paralyzing effects of anxiety—and for raising it above that level whenever possible—is universal. The behavioral consequences of such motivation depend upon the strategies for management of self-esteem that individuals select: adjusting behavior to the expectations of significant others, seeking significant others who will provide favorable evaluations, and, evaluating oneself in ways that either reinforce an already attained level of self-esteem (whether high or low) by virtue of the development of autonomy, or cause a retreat into fantasy. The second proposition links commitment to social norms with development of adequate self-esteem. When group reinforcement for self-esteem is lacking, the individual will not develop commitment to the group's norms. When self-esteem is seriously threatened, already developed commitment will be correspondingly damaged. The specific behavioral consequences depend upon the variety of group contexts available, the relative balance between threats to and supports for self-esteem in such contexts, and the norms of each. The third proposition links self-esteem with anxiety and with the individual's capacity to sustain interpersonal relations. Specific behavioral consequences depend upon the level of self-esteem and on the specific ways in which anxiety and interpersonal difficulties affect existing normative commitments, relationships, and strivings for self-esteem.

It is very important that we understand that these three basic ways in which self-esteem influences behavior are mutually interactive; the behavioral consequences implied by any one of the propositions have their own implications for self-esteem and for the variables of the other propositions. For example, a person's ability to choose confirming significant others, and thus to maintain or improve his self-esteem, depends upon his ability to carry on rewarding interpersonal relationships. One of the concomitants of low self-esteem— anxiety and interpersonal difficulties—interferes directly with the individual's ability to find and get along with others who might improve his self-esteem. Furthermore, if reduced self-esteem leads to reduced commitment and nonconforming behavior, resulting negative evaluations can produce further losses of self-esteem. Such feedback can be vicious: The school child does poorly in his academic work, and the resulting negative appraisals lower his self-esteem, possibly reducing his commitment to the norms that call upon him to succeed academically, which in turn may lead to even poorer performance, more negative evaluations, and further reductions in commitment. As the child grows older, his self-image develops in terms of academic incompetence, and he tends to reinforce low self-esteem with self-evaluations. It is possible, of course, for a child to insulate himself against negative appraisals of his academic work and to learn to like himself despite others' low evaluations of him. Doing so, however, requires at least some assistance from outside (like parents, who, in wanting him to do well, tell him that he is really quite able), and also perhaps a considerable retreat from reality.

These links between self-esteem and behavior are also positively interactive. The progressive development of commitments to social norms along with the development of self-esteem implies that the person is able to find a network of other people with whom to interact, with whom to seek and grant approval, and with whom he can define himself. As the process goes on, the person becomes more and more socially autonomous, and finds reinforcements for self-esteem and normative commitments within himself as well as in the responses of others.

This process is shaped and limited by an important feature of social structure. During childhood socialization, when most of the self is formed, several alternative sources of group support for self-esteem are usually available. The child has access to multiple interaction contexts: family, schools, peers, and other adults. If self-esteem is attacked in one context, the child may seek to bolster it in another. The fact that most people have such a variety of contexts of interaction to which they can turn means that most of them can develop adequate self-esteem by participating in contexts of interaction and behaving in accord with precepts that are most rewarding.

Self-Esteem and Deviant Behavior

The desire for self-esteem thus channels energy into forms of behavior and patterns of interpersonal relationships that permit the individual to build and maintain it. The propositions that we have formulated enable us to construct a model of the "normal" process of socialization: As children grow into adults, they move from early situations in which self-esteem is based on positive appraisals by adults whose expectations they have met to later situations in which the children choose significant others to reinforce established self-images. In this process, they develop commitments to social norms, learn how to interact with others, and build self-esteem. Some norms are internalized. Other norms, though they have attracted commitment, require a continuing flow of rewards to ensure conforming behavior. The individual can interact with others in order to satisfy his basic physiological and psychological needs, he has the skills necessary to play the roles he is called upon to play, and he shares a common language and a common set of cultural meanings with other members of his society and groups.[12]

Deviant behavior occurs when social arrangements interfere with this "normal" process of socialization—that is, when the development and maintenance of adequate self-esteem are inhibited. In the remainder of this chapter we shall deal with the contexts of interaction that are most important in socialization and with the kinds of interference with development of self-esteem that they may impose. Our fundamental thesis is that any society contains at least some social arrangements in which participation is either normative or unavoidable, yet that so inhibit development of adequate self-esteem as to produce poorly socialized people.

In a modern society three contexts of social interaction are of paramount importance in socialization: the private family setting; more complex public settings like schools, religious organizations, social-service agencies, and clubs, of which the most important is the public school; and those provided by peers (others of the same or similar age with whom interaction is frequent and between whom there is mutual influence and identification) with whom children identify on the basis of age and sex. The context we have called "private" may include, in addition to the nuclear family unit, a collection of other relatives; sometimes it includes unrelated individuals who share the family's residence or who live close to the family and perform some of the same functions as do family members in the socialization of the child. For example, neighbors and honorary "aunts" are frequently included in the private family circle. The public context includes official and quasi-official agencies that assume some responsibility for socialization, with or without the cooperation of parents. Policemen, social workers, youth workers, and religious functionaries are some of those who may contribute to the public socialization of the young. From available children, every child selects a limited circle of those who share not only a similar age status (although the age range of peer groups can vary considerably), but who possess other characteristics that encourage frequent interaction and mutual influence and indentification.

The private realm occupies a special, powerful place among these three arenas of socialization. During his first years the child spends most of his time in the company of his family, with whom strong affective ties have usually been established. (The term "affect" or "affective" refers to the pleasurable or painful reactions to objects, people, or events, including reactions—such as "anger," "love," "fear," "liking," and "hate"— that are often called "emotions.") The relevant distinction is between "affective" and "cognitive," which is roughly parallel to the common distinction drawn between "feeling" and "thinking." Affect is, however, a more general concept than emotion. The experiences of the child within the private sphere critically influence his later experiences in more public spheres and his reactions to them.

Not that the child's experiences and adjustments within the family necessarily fix the pattern of his entire life unalterably.[13] It is more accurate to say that a person's childhood experiences set boundaries on his future social behavior. The orientations and adjustments that the child makes restrict his choices in adolescence and adulthood. For example, if a child learns very early that his self-esteem depends upon excelling in academic pursuits, he is likely to carry this orientation into adolescence and adulthood. An early set of commitments to such pursuits is very likely to become part of the autonomous standards that the adult uses to evaluate himself.

The family may erect a variety of obstacles to the child's self-esteem. In the "normal" socialization process that we have described the child is exposed to progressively more demanding normative expectations as he grows older; we expect more of six-year-olds than of two-year-olds. When our expectations are met the child is rewarded with praise, for example; failure to meet them results in criticism. The family may disrupt this "normal" process, however, in a number of different ways. First, it may fail to make clear to the child its normative expectations. Second, it may present him with conflicting normative expectations, calling upon him to live up to norms that are mutually contradictory. As a result it may sometimes reward and sometimes punish the child for the same behavior. Third, it may fail to reward behavior in accordance with its norms. Fourth, the family may establish a tone of neutral or negative affect in all its dealings with the child regardless of how well he conforms to normative expectations.

These obstacles to self-esteem and the development of normative commitments fall into two categories. The first four involve evaluation of *behavior* and undermine the child's efforts to construct a behavioral logic for himself. A behavioral logic is a coherent frame of reference, based on the expectations and activities of the parents, in terms of which the child can judge his own behavior. For example, the child who has done very well in school should be able to count on the approval of his parents and relate it to their expectations of him. He needs a measure of coherence among expectations, behavior, and evaluations. The absence of such a behavioral logic means that the child will not always know why he is being positively or negatively evaluated or what is expected of him.

The fifth obstacle falls into a different category, involving the evaluation of the *child* rather than of his behavior. Socialization is most effective when it takes place in an atmosphere of positive affective ties with parents. Learning and cognition are not independent of the affective conditions under which they take place, and when the climate of socialization is painful to the child his learning is likely to be impeded. If the family environment is affectively negative, the development of normative commitments and self-esteem is retarded: fear, anxiety, and dislike are inimical to the construction of self-esteem.

Because one or more of these obstacles may be present, children do not always emerge from their families with adequate self-esteem. There are individual differences in levels of self-esteem, in the ability to resist attacks upon self-esteem, in commitments to family norms, and in abilities to carry on interpersonal relations satisfactorily. A child's entry into public socialization contexts severely tests his developing self and draws heavily upon its resources, for these public contexts provide the possibility of further barriers to development of adequate self-esteem.

The task of public agents of socialization is to expand and refine normative commitments developed earlier within the family and to develop specialized skills in preparation for adult status. (The question of how successfully these public agents perform this task for various segments of the society is taken up in Chapter 3.) The school, for example, provides the opportunity to learn new norms, skills, and information. The child learns to read, write, and count; becomes familiar with the history and traditions of his society; and learns to interact with new and different kinds of people. Such tasks may not be accomplished smoothly, however, if his self-esteem is seriously threatened or impaired.

Public obstacles to self-esteem fall into the same categories as private ones. In some cases, the child may be unable to construct a behavioral logic in public contexts, or he may be unable to use the one previously constructed in the family. The school, in much the same way as the family, can fail to make its normative expectations clear. But even if it does make them clear, they may be inconsistent with those standards he has learned in his family. For example, the culture of the school is orderly and controlled by time, whereas many children who enter it have not been previously taught to value punctuality. A child whose life is regulated by impulse—who has been fed whenever he was hungry, for example—may fail to perceive the urgency of doing homework assignments on time. In addition, the school may impose standards of etiquette that are foreign to the child. This child may thus encounter adults whose standards he cannot meet, and even if he were to meet them in public contexts, he would not necessarily be rewarded for doing so. In such contexts, the distribution of rewards is sometimes controlled by considerations that are not germane to the child's behavior. Lower-class children may find, for example, that they do not receive approval even when their behavior is normative, because their social class influences their teachers' appraisals of them.

On the other hand, regardless of the degree to which his behavior conforms to the expectations of the adults who control these public contexts, the child may be evaluated by ascriptive standards that he cannot alter. To be a black child in the public world of whites is to experience repeatedly the denigration of his color, sometimes through direct statements, sometimes more subtle expression of attitudes. Either way the climate is one of negative affect.

In public contexts of socialization, as in the family, negative evaluations of the self unrelated to behavioral expectations are especially damaging to self-esteem because they create anxiety that is difficult to manage. The black child cannot alter his color or his parents and their color. When an ascribed characteristic is negatively evaluated, the child can find no behavioral logic to guide him in avoiding such evaluation in the future. He may attempt to withdraw from contexts in which he is so rated, but withdrawal is frequently impossible, as with the school. The black child may refrain from involvement in school activities and refuse to accept negative evaluations in that context, but he must continue to attend or suffer serious penalties, both immediate and delayed.

We may summarize this description of socialization in the following proposition: The balance of threats to and supports for self-esteem that the child receives in various public and private contexts of socialization, together with the normative orientations that each context encourages, determines the normative and behavioral directions that the child will take as he grows into adulthood. The less secure the self-esteem of the child when he moves from the private sphere into public contexts, the shakier it will become in those contexts. At one extreme is the child whose self-esteem is wholly inadequate, who is beset by enormous anxiety, whose normative commitments are weak if they exist at all, and who is not well enough disposed toward others to interact with them successfully. Assuming that such a child is capable of functioning in a social group (which is doubtful), his experiences in public contexts will determine whether his self-esteem will be damaged irreparably or will be built up to the point of adequacy. The former is more probable, and the result may be some form of mental illness. At the other extreme is the child whose self-esteem is more than adequate, who is committed to his family's norms, who can interact successfully with others, and who can easily manage any anxieties that arise.

The majority of children fall between these extremes, and the normative orientations and self-esteem that they develop after they leave the exclusive context of the family are functions of the degree of consistency between the norms they have learned in the family and those to which they are exposed in public contexts; the affective quality of their experiences in public contexts; their ability to manage anxiety resulting from threats to self-esteem in public contexts; and the capacity of the family to provide emotional and evaluative support when self-esteem is threatened in public contexts of socialization.

Peer groups are important in socialization, but they cannot by themselves provide "normal" socialization. That is, the child cannot find within the peer group sufficient support for his self-esteem or sufficient help in developing role skills, cognitive abilities, and interpersonal capacities. The socializing power of the peer group is limited by its subjection to the power of adult society; adults watch and exert control over the activities of juveniles. Furthermore, as children are relatively unsocialized themselves, they cannot socialize one another as effectively as the family or school can.

The peer group is not, however, unimportant in the socialization of its members. Often it reinforces the normative commitments developed in the family context. Other such commitments are challenged by a child's friends; most children now and then bring home friends whose values and normative commitments are at odds with their own and whom their parents dislike. The important question is whether or not they remain friends, and the answer depends upon the family's ability to make adherence to its norms more rewarding to the child than his friendship with someone whom his parents dislike. Ordinarily there are strong presures for children to associate with peers whose normative orientations are similar to those of significant adults. When a child can find no adult context of socialization that permits him to develop adequate self-esteem, however, he will try to bolster his self-esteem exclusively in the company of peers. But he will very likely fail. The problem of total dependence upon peers for reinforcement of self-esteem will be considered extensively in the next chapter.

How may deviant behavior emerge from the quest for self-esteem? In anticipation of a more detailed analysis in subsequent chapters, we offer the following outline.

First, in his quest for significant others to bolster his self-esteem the child may attach himself to those who will provide favorable evaluations of behavior that is socially defined as deviant. He may become attached to a *deviant subculture* of one kind or another.

Second, if the child finds no significant adults to assist him in the task of building self-esteem, his commitment to norms may be so low, his ability to function interpersonally so damaged, and his detachment from adult society so thorough that he comes to depend exclusively upon his peers for support of his self-esteem. In their company he is likely to become involved in situations in which deviant behavior is precipitated and tolerated.

Third, if the child reaches adulthood with only marginal self-esteem, he will be constantly sensitive to threats to it and therefore susceptible to further reductions in already low normative commitments and interpersonal capacities. Under such conditions deviant behavior may occur from time to time, and mental disorder may develop.

Fourth, if the child's self-esteem is so inadequate that his major adjustments to life involve retreats from interpersonal relationships, then his behavior is probably characterized by some form of mental disorder.

Self-Esteem and Social Stratification

In this book we have placed considerable emphasis upon the sociological concept of evaluation. In our discussion of social stratification we stressed the process of differential evaluation. And in our discussion of self-esteem we have stressed the influence of evaluations of behavior in the formation of self-esteem. We can, at this stage, begin to bring together the three major themes in our discussion up to this point: stratification, self-esteem, and deviant behavior.

Social stratification is linked to deviant behavior through the mechanism of self-esteem. A person's position in the social system, because it subjects him to differential evaluation, affects the development of his self-esteem, and serious interference may lead to deviant behavior. The concept of evaluation is central both to stratification and to the development of self-esteem; because behavioral orientations hinge upon levels of self-esteem they also hinge upon positions in the system of social inequalities.

An individual's social position determines the evaluations he receives in several ways, especially in concrete interaction contexts; it also influences the kinds of people whom he can regard as significant and who will reciprocate his regard, as well as the level of prestige he can claim. Membership in a social stratum implies life styles—for example, modes of behavior related to family patterns—that may themselves determine a person's ability to develop self-esteem. Some deviant behavior arises because those whose self-esteem is most threatened in public differential evaluation are also most likely to come from families that are unable to provide their own kinds of support for self-esteem. Life chances are also important: Frequently the effects of low prestige and inadequate family supports are compounded by inadequate opportunities for health, employment, and financial security. Such poor life chances reinforce low self-esteem by providing the individual with evidence that he can easily interpret as demonstrating his lack of worth.

The effect of social stratification on self-esteem is thus three-fold: Differential evaluation acts directly on self-esteem. Family life styles associated with social position affect ability to manage self-esteem. And, finally, life chances provide tangible evidence of individual worth. In subsequent chapters we shall explore in detail several specific sets of circumstances in which deviant behavior results from the impact of social inequalities on striving for adequate self-esteem.

Notes

1. Symbolic interactionism is a theoretical perspective within sociology and social psychology that emphasizes the "inner" aspects of human behavior. It concerns itself with such matters as the role of symbolic communication in human behavior and the formation of the self in social interaction. A useful and sophisticated collection of articles on symbolic interactionism may be found in Jerome G. Manis and Bernard N. Meltzer (eds.), *Symbolic Interaction: A Reader in Social Psychology* (Boston: Allyn and Bacon, 1967). See also Anselm Strauss, ed., *George Herbert Mead: On Social Psychology* (Chicago: University of Chicago Press, 1964).
2. Strauss, *op. cit.*, p. 202.
3. Morris Rosenberg, *Society and the Adolescent Self-Image* (Princeton, N.J.: Princeton University Press, 1965), pp. 5–8.
4. The qualifying term "normally" is necessary in order to allow for masochists, who persist in inflicting physical or psychic harm upon themselves. To assert that the pursuit of self-esteem is normal is to imply that masochism is pathological.
5. Much of the following discussion is based on Hans Gerth and C. Wright Mills, *Character and Social Structure* (New York: Harcourt, 1953).
6. *Ibid.*, p. 85.
7. *Ibid.*, p. 87.
8. Melvin Tumin, "Business as a Social System," *Behavioral Science*, 9 (1964), 129.
9. Harry Stack Sullivan, *The Interpersonal Theory of Psychiatry* (New York: Norton, 1953), p. 351.
10. Rosenberg, op. cit., pp. 168–187.
11. Ibid., pp. 18–30, 153–159.
12. See Jack L. Roach and O. Gurrslin, "The Lower-Class, Status Frustration and Social Disorganization," *Social Forces*, 43 (1965), 501–509.
13. See J. Milton Yinger, *Toward a Field Theory of Behavior* (New York: McGraw-Hill, 1965).

Lower-Straum Subcultures and Lower-Stratum Juveniles

3

In this chapter we examine the participation of lower-stratum Americans in the system of social stratification and its effects upon their self-esteem and behavior. We begin with an analysis of lower-stratum subcultures, attempting to identify the normative, coercive, and situational factors governing the behavior of their members.

The Nature of Lower-Stratum Subcultures

The term "lower-stratum subcultures" rests upon prior understanding of the differences between "lower stratum" and "middle stratum." The line between these categories is roughly that between manual and nonmanual occupations. Occupation, as we saw in Chapter 2, is a major criterion of prestige in American society, and there is an enduring tendency in the United States to evaluate manual occupations as less worthwhile than nonmanual ones. Of course, such a distinction on the basis of any single criterion is somewhat arbitrary. But the perfect division of American society into prestige strata is impossible because there are many criteria of prestige allocation on which lack of consensus is frequent and because there is no widely accepted formula for adding up units of prestige attributed according to the various criteria. The use of the manual-nonmanual distinction to distinguish two social strata reflects the fact that occupation is the most widely accepted of all the criteria of prestige allocation.

The lower stratum consists of families whose *heads* have manual occupations. An understanding of the subcultures within the stratum requires an examination of the variations in life styles and life chances within it, and that is by no means an easy task. In addition to variations in occupation, income, and prestige, there are variations in region, religion, ethnic affiliation, race, family tradition, community size, personal aspirations, and individual self-identifications. Lower-stratum subcultures differ from one part of the country to another because of regional differences in the origins and traditions of lower-stratum groups. Some subcultures have arisen indigenously in the course of economic development, some have risen among slaves imported to work plantations, some have risen among immigrant laborers in expanding industrial society. Furthermore, any discussion of lower-stratum people must carefully identify differences among those who are willing and permanent members of the stratum; those who seek upward social mobility but have not yet attained it; those who have been left behind as others of their ethnic or historical origins rose out of the stratum; those who have fallen from higher social status; and those who ordinarily hold non-manual jobs but currently have a manual job, perhaps because of temporary employment difficulties.

We can then cautiously identify two major subcultures, which form the bulk of the lower stratum. The life styles of the subcultures are different, and the life chances of their members are unequal. By "life chances" we mean the typical chances of an individual to survive past any given age, to enjoy mental and physical health, to acquire the skills necessary to physical and psychic survival, and to pass such important milestones as high school graduation, the acquisition of higher education, marriage, obtaining a job, regular career advancements, and so on. Life styles are social perspectives whose development is encouraged by life chances and the institutional practices in which they result. Social perspectives may be defined as fundamental beliefs about experience, life, and society, including views on justice and on the likelihood that men receive their just dues, trust in the motives and actions of others, and belief in the possibility of rational planning for the future. Institutional practices are the typical ways in which men perform within the major institutions of their society: how they define and serve their gods, raise children, participate in political activities, take recreation, consume, express beliefs, make love, learn, define and discover truth, and so forth. Life chances may be viewed as operating through social perspectives to encourage the development of certain institutional practices. In American society, life chances are distributed unequally according to social position; although there are compensating mechanisms that soften the effects of such inequalities, considerable differences in life styles do exist both within and among the major strata.

Herbert Gans has described the behavioral differences between lower-stratum and middle-stratum members of the society in terms of the organization, stability, and outlook of the family.[1] The lower-stratum person perceives the family as a secure retreat from the hostile outside world, which he believes will subordinate his interests to its own if he is not careful. A member of the middle stratum, however, is less likely to perceive a hostile world outside the protective sanctuary of the family. While members of this stratum often feel threatened by outsiders, their response is not to withdraw to the family circle, but to seek the company and the ideological support of other members of their stratum. The threats they perceive may come from ethnic groups that seem to threaten their social position or their safety or from the power of government, which they often see as a threat to their autonomy and privilege, and so on. One might say that the middle-stratum people are oriented to a defense of privilege, whereas the lower-stratum people are oriented to a defense against privilege. As a result, middle-stratum people define outsiders in terms of their stratum's boundaries, but lower-stratum people define them in terms of a smaller circle of relatives and close friends.

Lower-stratum people regard the family unit as central to life's activities and as an essential defense against the outside world. Within the lower stratum, however, there are important differences in life chances and life styles that divide it into two major subcultures, which for convenience we shall designate as the *lower class* and the *working class*. (The term "class" as used here does not refer to a self-conscious unit of social organization with common goals and collective actions to attain them but rather to a unit defined by its participation in a more or less common subculture. The term "subculture" is applied to normative precepts and life styles that are shared by some, but not all, of the members of a society, and that differ in important respects from those of others. Frequently those who participate in a subculture share the political and economic orientations of the rest of society but not their religion or style of family life, and often the normative precepts and life styles that mark the existence of a subculture have emerged in opposition to those of the dominant culture.[2])

The working-class subculture is dominated by the family unit—the circle of relatives, however closely or loosely defined. "Its way of life is based on social relationships amongst relatives. The working-class views the world from the family circle, and considers everything outside it as either a means to its maintenance or to its destruction."[3] S. M. Miller and Frank Riessman have characterized the cultural orientations of the working class in terms of a few basic themes.[4] One such theme is the search for security and stability, which is related to such issues in working-class family life as unemployment and layoff, family discord, intergenerational conflict, and the need and desire for excitement, all of which promote insecurity and instability. The working-class family tends also to support traditional values that differentiate it from the middle class, partly because large proportions of the working class are descended from immigrants and retain many of their traditional cultural values. Working-class members prefer to relate to people than to roles and bureaucratic structures. The subculture is pragmatic, emphasizing the results of action and placing low value upon abstract thought; it tends to be somewhat anti-intellectual.

The working-class subculture differs significantly from the lower-class subculture. The most important difference is in family organization: Although both working-class and lower-class subcultures emphasize the importance of the family, the lower-class family is to a great extent dominated by and organized around women.[5] Males are neither dominant nor stable members of the household; they provide sexual services and some economic support but play little part in raising children, in organizing the family and making its decisions, and in affective transactions within the family circle.

There is another important difference: Much behavior in the lower-class subculture is not regulated by traditional normative commitments but by learned and culturally transmitted responses to situational demands and to the coercive expectations of others. To put it very simply, lower-class people face major problems of adjustment and survival, and they frequently behave as they do because they must. The behavior that characterizes the lower-class subculture does not result simply from a set of norms. High rates of mental illness, crowded living conditions, illegitimacy, loosely structured mating relationships, school-dropout rates, and mistreatment of children do not usually result from normative commitments but represent responses (whether adaptive or not) to the demands of the lower-class situation.

The life chances of men in the lower class are marked by marginal employment and minimum economic security, so that their deprivation is severe, not only relative to the rest of the society but in absolute terms as well. The minimum resources necessary to sustain adequate health, to provide children with opportunities to secure as much education as their abilities will allow, or even to develop those abilities, to maintain family stability, and to preserve psychic integrity are frequently not available. The lower class thus makes the poorest showing of any major social group on a large number of indicators of social pathology, such as mental illnesses, physical health, family disorganization, and so on.[6]

We are interested in the effects of such subcultural differences and characteristics upon the participation of lower-class and working-class Americans in the process of differential evaluation; we begin by focusing our attention on the juvenile members of the two subcultures. First in their families and later in public socialization contexts, juveniles encounter evaluations that are influenced by their parents' positions in the system of social inequalities.

Subcultural Experiences and Threats to Self-Esteem

The degree to which the child is sensitive to threats to his self-esteem in public contexts depends upon the adequacy of his self-esteem as developed within the family. The less adequate his self-esteem when he leaves the exclusive protection of his family, the greater his difficulties in public are likely to be. The differences between the lower class and the working class that we have outlined imply systematic differences in self-esteem between lower-class and working-class children as well. The lower-class child is more likely to have been socialized in an unstable family, often without a male head; in an affectively negative environment; and without a clear and consistent set of norms in terms of which he can build his self-esteem.

It is not difficult to show that the lower class is a major population group, although it is nearly impossible to give a precise estimate of its size. If we use families headed by women as a basic, though crude, indicator of the size of the lower class, we find that some 9.3 percent of the more than 45 million families in the United States in 1960 were headed by women. Since some of these families were presumably middle-class families that lost a male head by death, separation, or divorce, not all families headed by women can be considered lower-class families. But data show that the median income of families headed by women ($3,401) is almost half that of families headed by men ($5,901). Among blacks, a population group that is disproportionately concentrated in the lower class (with 84.6 percent employed in manual occupations as compared to 52.6 percent of whites, and with unemployment rates that are frequently more than double those of whites), fully 21 percent of all families were headed by women.[7]

Another indicator of the size of the lower class is income. Lower-class people are on the low and unstable end of the distribution of income. Herman Miller found just over 10 million families below a poverty line of $3,000 in 1960, which constitutes somewhat more than the lowest fifth of the income distribution.[8] All who are poor by this standard, however, are not necessarily lower-class, as we have defined the term. Some of those who earn less than the $3,000 poverty line are the aged, many of whom are working-class or middle-class in all but income, and some are middle-class and working-class female heads of families who have lost their male head through divorce, desertion, or death, but who maintain their norms and patterns of behavior.

Another indicator is the use of welfare statistics as a measure of the size of the hard core lower-class. Of the nearly 4 million adults and children relieved by the Aid to Families with Dependent Children Program in 1963 (nearly all of whom were women and children), representing 910,000 families, two-thirds of the fathers were absent because they were never married to the mother (as is true in a fifth of the cases), or due to divorce, legal separation, desertion, or imprisonment. Matza argues that between 25 and 45 percent of these AFDC families may be deemed disreputable by general community standards, judging from the fact that they remain unemployed even during periods of general prosperity and relatively full employment. Slightly more than 50 percent of the AFDC families in 1963 had been receiving assistance for more than two years.[9]

However, such figures must be treated cautiously. Since the AFDC programs are used disproportionately by nonwhites (mostly blacks), the numbers of white people in the lower class may be underestimated. These figures also do not represent those people who may be eligible but who do not use public welfare programs, and those who just barely fail to qualify for assistance due to residence requirements, which were recently declared unconstitutional by the Supreme Court, or because they are employed, even though they earn substandard wages. In addition to the above-mentioned disreputable poor and welfare poor are simply the poor, many of whom are lower-class by virtue of economic uncertainty, marginality, and family disorganization, and whose numbers it is almost impossible to establish.

What are the effects of lower-class membership on self-esteem? Can we relate those variables which we have regarded as central to the lower-class/working-class dichotomy, (family disorganization and female domination) to levels of self-esteem? Are there any connections between the socialization practices of families, as differentiated by social class, and the level of self-esteem developed in their children? Two recent studies provide important data.

Rosenberg's study of self-attitudes among 5,024 high school juniors and seniors in New York State demonstrated a relationship between social class and self-esteem. Using a seven-point scale to measure self-esteem and an index of social class based on fathers' median incomes, education, and source of income, Rosenberg found that 38 percent of those in the lowest class (whose fathers were mostly manual laborers or service workers who had not progressed beyond grade school) were "high" in self-esteem as compared to 51 percent of those in the highest class.[10] He also found that boys with lower-class fathers were more likely to have lower self-esteem than girls.[11]

The main defect of Rosenberg's data concerns his sampling procedures. The sample was confined to juniors and seniors in high school and, therefore, since there is an inverse relationship between income and the tendency to drop out, the sample is biased toward working-class and middle-class adolescents who did not drop out.[12] We cannot know what social-class effects upon self-esteem would have been uncovered had the sample been more representative of the class structure, but, on the basis of trends in the existing data, it seems plausible to argue that even more pronounced effects would have been found. Some specific findings that attempt to relate socialization practices to levels of self-esteem support this view.[13]

One of the factors that apparently accounts for social class differences in self-esteem, even in Rosenberg's biased sample, is the degree to which fathers are supportive. Apparently, middle-class sons have higher self-esteem in part because their fathers relate more closely and supportively to them.[14] Here, again, it would be better to know about degrees of supportiveness in lower-class family relationships. But, since one of the main attributes of lower-class families is the frequent or permanent absence of the father, it seems reasonable to conclude that, if data were available, they would show lower-class boys to have lower self-esteem than working-class boys at least in part because of the smaller likelihood of a close, supportive relationship with their fathers.

What other evidence is available? Rosenberg examined the impact of broken homes upon self-esteem and found a small overall relationship: children of divorced parents are less likely (by seven percentage points) to be in the highest self-esteem category and more likely (by eight percentage points) to be in the lowest categories. The relationships between self-esteem and divorce are stronger when the child is Catholic or Jewish rather than Protestant; when the divorce took place when the mother was young; and when the mother remarried.[15] Unfortunately, data are not provided to show the relationship between social class, divorce, and self-esteem, which, in addition to the under-representation of lower-class people in the sample, makes it difficult to draw conclusions about divorce and self-esteem. We cannot know if the effects are more pronounced for members of the lower class. In any case, since divorce may actually be viewed as a favorable alternative to a negative family climate, statistics of divorce are likely to be somewhat misleading as a measure of the impact of family disorganization.

The study also found that parental interest is a major variable affecting self-esteem. Using several measures of parental interest in the child (including responses to questions like "How often do you participate in mealtime conversation?" and "As far as you can tell, how interested are the other family members in what you have to say on such occasions?") Rosenberg found that adolescents for whom there was no evidence of lack of interest on the part of parents were twenty percent more likely to have "high" self-esteem than those for whom there was some evidence of lack of parental interest.[16]

A more recent study confirms and elaborates many of Rosenberg's findings. Stanley Coopersmith conducted an extensive study of 85 preadolescents, all of whom were male, white, and "normal" (exhibiting no evidence of serious emotional disturbance), although few were working-class or lower-class.[17] Coopersmith found the same weak relationship between what he called "social class" (a classification based on the subject's scores on a combined index of father's income and occupation) and self-esteem. His "lower-class" respondents were somewhat more likely to have low self-esteem than his higher-class respondents.[18] But, because of his exclusion of the lowest class, Coopersmith's findings understate whatever relationships may really exist between self-esteem and social class. Coopersmith's study, like Rosenberg's, makes the unwarranted assumption that if social class is significant for self-esteem, there should be a direct positive relationship between the two. It is better not to make this assumption; the propositions we have developed suggest class differentials in a number of obstacles to the pursuit of self-esteem but do not imply any necessary differentials in the *outcome* of self-esteem for members of different social classes, except for those in the lower class. In this connection, it should be noted that Coopersmith's data do reveal that fathers with histories of unemployment are more likely to have sons with low self-esteem.[19] The significance of this finding is that unstable employment is a lower-stratum—especially a lower-class—characteristic.

Bearing in mind the limitations of his sample, Coopersmith's data also bear out some of Rosenberg's findings and our expectations about the relationships between the climate and organization of the family and self-esteem. Low self-esteem was found to be related to a history of one or more marriages previous to the present one on the part of either a boy's father or his mother. Marked tension between parents was also related to low self-esteem in their sons. The mothers of boys with low self-esteem were less loving and less closely involved with their sons than the mothers of boys with high self-esteem. Finally, families in which parents made firm demands on their sons and enforced them carefully and warmly, stressing rewards rather than punishments, were more conducive to the development of high self-esteem than families in which parents failed to provide guidance and were harsh and disrespectful in their treatment of their sons.[20] While bearing in mind that Rosenberg and Coopersmith used predominately middle-class subjects, their findings suggest that many of the characteristics of lower-class and, to a lesser extent, working-class families are precisely the ones that can be related to low self-esteem.

Development of self-esteem is thus often seriously jeopardized by the family experiences of lower-class children, especially boys. When they leave the exclusive care of the family, both lower-class and working-class boys may face further obstacles to the construction or preservation of adequate self-esteem. In American society the public school is the single most important context in which the self-esteem of lower-stratum boys is tested.

What obstacles to the further development of self-esteem do lower-stratum children face in the public school? One possibility is direct evaluation as unworthy, unclean, and undesirable because of the social status of his parents. Such direct evaluations by teachers and other students may be both subtly and unsubtly expressed. The school adults, for example, may show disrespect toward the child and may make no effort to conceal the basis of their disrespect in the child's background. Academic accomplishments may be unfairly rewarded, so that the adequate or even outstanding performances of lower-stratum children receive less attention and praise than do similar performances by middle-stratum children. Teachers may favor middle-stratum children in the distribution of honorific titles and positions; they may form their expectations of their students' abilities according to parents' social status and refuse to allow those expectations to be altered by any evidence.

Probably very few teachers inform their lower-stratum students directly that they are dirty, stupid, and socially undesirable, although some clearly do just that. In fact, it should not be assumed that *all* teachers devalue their lower-stratum students: Many are quite sensitive to their students' struggles to build self-esteem, and as public awareness of the problem increases so will the number of such teachers. But, on the whole, it is probable that lower-stratum boys will encounter threats to self-esteem in the schools, and many will experience such threats severely and continually.

In addition to being rated low by the system and its representatives, the lower-stratum boy, if he takes the system seriously, may rate himself low. As Albert Cohen has suggested,[21] the lower-stratum boy is likely to feel shame to the degree that he cares what his middle-stratum teachers think of him. And, although the lower-stratum boy is somewhat protected by his resistance to developing commitment to people and norms that devalue him, he cannot remove himself completely from their influence or perhaps even totally escape attachment to them.

The self-esteem of lower-stratum boys may also be severely threatened because they cannot adequately satisfy the schools' rigorous middle-stratum expectations, for which they have not been previously equipped. This conclusion is inescapable in the light of numerous studies of cognitive and linguistic differences between lower- and middle-stratum children showing that the path of the lower-stratum child is harder because he cannot grasp, or can grasp only with difficulty, middle-stratum forms of expression and communication. Lower-stratum cognitive styles typically emphasize direct and unmodified expression and stress unquestioning adherence to rules; in contrast middle-stratum styles emphasize extensive use of qualifying adjectives and the explanation of rules and the reasons for their existence. Basil Bernstein's studies, among others, clearly show the linguistic evidence of these differences in cognitive styles:[22] Lower-stratum children use less elaborate grammatical constructions and find the more complex expression of middle-stratum teachers difficult to comprehend. If, for example, a child is accustomed to being told to "shut up," the suggestion that he would be "more considerate of others" if he made less noise may be difficult for him to understand. Such differences in language reflect deeper differences in the ways in which reality is structured and perceived. In this example the lower-stratum usage is based on authoritarian structure, whereas the middle-stratum usage is based on a more equalitarian structure in which rules must be explained.

The lower-stratum child has not been socialized to cope with middle-stratum forms of communication and understanding. Yet he can behave appropriately in lower-stratum situations, and often he can successfully fulfill complex and difficult behavioral requirements. For example, he may be able to wend his way through a complex maze of urban streets and subways, protect his own interests in an indifferent and sometimes hostile world, and in many ways adapt to situations that would bewilder a middle-stratum child. But when he must rise with dignity and explain, in tones and language acceptable to his middle-stratum teacher, what has happened to a character in a story about middle-stratum people, he is less likely to perform well. Such failures wound his dignity and sense of self-worth.

There is an abundance of empirical evidence for this fact. Studies have demonstrated that status differences create obstacles in the student-teacher relationship; that higher-status students receive more of the rewards and fewer of the punishments meted out in schools; that school systems are oriented toward middle stratum values and that the character reputations among teachers of adolescents depend upon their conformity to the middle-stratum ideology of the school; and that community status systems are reflected in school status systems.[23] There is also evidence that high self-esteem is associated with better-than-average academic performance; that level of self-esteem is directly related to the child's perception of the teacher's appraisal of him; and that perception of favorable appraisals by teachers is directly related to better academic performance and more "desirable" (that is, middle-stratum oriented) classroom behavior.[24]

What do the propositions developed in Chapter 2 enable us to predict about the behavioral consequences of obstacles to self-esteem? First, lower-stratum children continue their efforts to acquire self-esteem by searching for significant others within other contexts of socialization, since they have not found them within the school. Second, lower-class and working-class children are less likely than middle-class children to develop and maintain commitment to the norms of the school. Those norms emphasize achievement, the value of education, the need for hard work, respect for the authority of the school, and other typical middle-class values. Because their self-esteem is threatened in the context that provides their main contact with such norms, lower-stratum children do not often become committed to them. And third, to the extent that the school is actually able to damage self-esteem, lower-stratum children will exhibit higher levels of anxiety and suffer from a reduced capacity to get along with others.

There is evidence that such obstacles to self-esteem are more serious for boys than for girls. Recall that Rosenberg found the association between self-esteem and social class to be stronger for boys than for girls.[25] For the lower-class boy, the absence of a masculine role model whom he can approve, and the disorganized status of family norms, may make the school's obstacles more threatening than for the lower-class girl, who may find the family a rewarding place to turn. For the working-class boy, the school may be somewhat more threatening than for the working-class girl because its middle-class values conflict more seriously with working-class conceptions of the male role than the female role. Working-class boys are urged to define themselves in terms of their occupational aspirations, which are closely related to success in school. They are urged to commit themselves to the school, but the school itself creates obstacles to such commitments by evaluating the boy on the basis of his class background and by conducting its business in a language with which he may not feel entirely comfortable. Working-class girls may find it easier to meet the minimum requirements of their school role, retreating whenever they can to the family and to their peers, to whose norms they are urged to become committed. As a result, because the school is more central to the future occupational and social standing of the boy than of the girl, the obstacles to self-esteem that it erects are more significant for boys.

The Development of Behavioral Orientations

Lower-stratum children develop behavioral orientations as a result of their cumulative experiences in various private and public contexts of socialization. The term "behavioral orientations" means a child's fairly conscious conformity to the expectations of significant adults. Such orientations eventually become consistent to the extent that any child can be characterized in terms of them. Obviously, however, a child's orientation toward certain expectations—his commitment to certain norms—indicates only his long-run tendency to conform to such norms. We can describe three possible behavioral orientations for lower-stratum youth.

These orientations, which are expressed primarily as attitudes toward present subcultural experiences and future employment, are mainly relevant to boys. Our emphasis on boys in this book is mostly due to the fact that self-esteem for boys is more closely tied to the stratification system than for girls. A man's worth in this society is judged, to a far greater extent than a woman's, by his accomplishments and position in the working world. Consequently, the connections between stratification, self-esteem, and behavior (both deviant and conforming) are probably more important for men than for women. Even though girls may be affected by prestige, boys find that, in growing up, their self-esteem is more intimately linked with social stratification than girls'.

The first of the behavioral orientations is the tendency of some lower-stratum youths to seek to escape their own subcultures by adopting the norms and values of middle-stratum subcultures, which emphasize achievement and success. They attribute to the life styles of their families and to the occupations of their fathers all the undesirable elements in their own experience and conclude that they must escape.

Second, some—perhaps most—lower-stratum youths have conscious, positive orientations toward their own subcultures. Such orientations do not encourage social mobility or indeed any kind of change that would involve associating with new significant groups and giving up subcultural loyalties. These boys see the middle-stratum world as threatening and undesirable but find the life styles of their families satisfying and meaningful.

Third, some adolescents develop no significant behavioral orientations toward adult norms. As far as social interaction and personal loyalties are concerned, they turn almost exclusively to their peers, and their rejection of adults and adult norms, if not complete or final, is at least substantial. The chances are greatest, as we shall see in more detail later, that they will become oriented to peers who also reject adults and adult norms. They see the adult world—its personnel and roles—as threatening, and they withdraw from it.

The balance of threats and supports from different contexts of socialization, together with the norms each context supports, determine which orientations the child develops. Our task is to understand how this proposition works in concrete terms—how, for example, the lower-stratum child develops an orientation toward social mobility.

Although one might suppose that upward mobility is everyone's goal—that everyone wants to be "better off" in possessions and prestige than he is—some people have limited aspirations for mobility out of their subcultures. The reasons for such limited aspirations are diverse, including positive attachment to the subculture, fear of taking the risks required by attempts to be mobile, and, quite often, lack of knowledge of *how* to attain mobility. The rewards of a rich society are apparent everywhere—they can be seen in any store and on every television set—but the means to obtain them are less clear. The lower-stratum youth may realize, for example, the value of education in the pursuit of mobility, but he may have little idea what a college is like or how to get into one. He may have mistaken notions about occupational opportunities—not only in the well-paid jobs to which he might aspire but also in manual occupations as well.[26] In addition, if his self-esteem has been deflated by his school experiences he will be unable to support school norms or to regard his teachers as legitimate models after which to fashion his own life. His parents can provide only limited knowledge of the means to attain success, and their attitudes toward education may be ambivalent: Even if they perceive the value of education, they may believe that the middle-class school is hostile to them and their values. It is likely, therefore, that the lower-stratum child will seek material success but will less frequently strive for mobility out of the lower-stratum subculture and into new middle-stratum worlds. Nevertheless, some lower-stratum youths do want social mobility, and it is possible to discover who they are.

The lower-stratum youth who has become oriented toward mobility out of his subculture probably has not been exposed to serious devaluation by the school, and his self-esteem has probably not been seriously threatened. The implication is not that his lower-stratum background has *never* earned him negative evaluations but rather that such devaluations have not been frequent enough or severe enough to offset the self-esteem that he has gained by living up to the school's expectations. Furthermore, his socialization in the family was very likely compatible with school expectations, so that he has been *able* to live up to its expectations. He has learned to comprehend middle-stratum thought and communication, to do his work well and on time, adapt to middle-stratum etiquette, and to accept middle-stratum teachers as legitimate role models. When we find a lower-stratum child with serious mobility aspirations, we also usually find a lower-stratum family that has actively and successfully promoted them.[27] Clearly, such aspirations depend upon a net balance of positive evaluation of the child, upon consistent expectations by private and public agencies of socialization (mainly parents and teachers), and upon maintenance of self-esteem through strong commitments to their norms.

Mobility aspirations may also develop in other ways, however. For example, some lower-stratum children aspire to social mobility even without strong parental encouragement if their school performances have been exceptional and at least some teachers have made strenuous efforts on their behalf. Similarly, some children survive a fair amount of hostility in school if the level of parental support is exceptionally high. Although both parental and school supports are necessary, some degree less of one may be made up by more of the other. Both must rise above a certain threshold, however, if the mobility orientation is to develop: Unless both parental and school supports rise above a minimum level, the probability of mobility orientation remains low regardless of how high the supports are from either one. The absence of active resistance is probably the minimum level of support that is required. If the child is to develop a mobility orientation mainly on the strength of parental support, the school must not actively oppose him, even if it does not support him. If he is to develop the orientation on the strength of the support of the school, his parents at least must not actively oppose him.

Note that so far the child's chances for *successful mobility* have not been mentioned. His success is determined over a long span of time and is related, among other things, to his abilities, as well as to his selection of peers. Peers do not themselves have enough influence to encourage genuine normative commitments, but they do have some power, especially when very little is required to tip the balance of a child's energies in one direction or another. Parental wishes can influence the selection of friends, but, of course, so can such chance factors as the kinds of associates available. Middle-stratum friends are also important to the mobility of the lower-stratum child because they greatly enhance his fund of knowledge, encouragement, and self-esteem.

Perhaps the most typical pattern for lower-stratum youth is a stable, lower-stratum subcultural orientation in which there is no desire for the prestige of middle-stratum groups, even though there is desire for material advancement. Generally the lower-stratum family does not encourage social mobility, and the lower-stratum child does not develop within his family the abilities and attitudes that might bring him success in school. The lower-stratum boy therefore tends to be devalued by the school—although the extent depends upon his family background, upon the nature of his school and its class composition, and upon his ability to adapt to the situation and make the best of it until he leaves school. If he is devalued, he is unlikely to become committed to the school and its norms. Instead, he turns still more to the family as a continuing warm source of support for his self-esteem and becomes more deeply committed to its norms. His peers also tend to have lower-stratum subcultural orientations, partly because he and his family gravitate toward people of similar orientations and partly because middle-stratum children and their families do the same.

Finally, some lower-stratum boys become oriented neither toward social mobility nor toward continuing membership in the lower-stratum subcultures of their parents because they are unable to maintain adequate self-esteem. For these boys the public agencies of socialization have been hostile and demeaning, and their families, by virtue either of disorganization or an affectively negative climate, have failed to provide enough positive support to offset the damage to self-esteem experienced in public. Many such boys are able to find no adults to act as significant others, and they turn exclusively to their peers. In the company of peers their behavior depends not upon the pursuit of conventional normative commitments or social mobility but upon a variety of complex situational factors and the dynamics of the group situation.

The chances that lower-class children will develop any one of these three behavioral orientations differ from those among working-class children. The lower-class child is more likely to suffer serious devaluation of his performances, possessions, positions, and attributes by the school—and is therefore more likely than his working-class peers to be adjudged *disreputable*.[28] He is less likely to present the kind of personal and social image respected by middle-class teachers, and he is much less likely to do well in terms of purely academic criteria. At the same time he is less likely to find within his family and its lower-class subculture a viable set of behavioral norms and group supports alternative to those of the school. Lower-class life—which, we have noted, is marked by unstable adult employment, greater family instability and disorganization, fewer positive norms for the guidance of behavior, weaker group supports for normative behavior, and more mental disorder—does not easily provide a basis for development and maintenance of adequate self-esteem. Consequently, the lower-class child is less likely than the working-class child to find any adult context of socialization within which self-esteem can be constructed. He is more likely to turn exclusively to the company of his peers. At school he finds people who let him know that he is stupid, lazy, dirty, and incompetent and make it clear that their evaluations are related to his family background, including color and ethnic origins. He seeks solace within the family but frequently does not find it; instead he is likely to find too little praise for his accomplishments, an unclear notion of what is expected of him, no clear notion of what it is to be a man, and often inattention and lack of interest from adults. Finding no reason to think well of himself in the company of adults, he turns to his peers.

The working-class child is considerably better off. He *may* face equally powerful threats to self-esteem in public contexts of socialization, but he is less likely to do so. He comes closer to satisfying the requirements and expectations of the school in its standards of performance, both academic and nonacademic. Indeed, his parents may subscribe to the norms of the school, urge his adherence to them, and encourage his mobility aspirations. He is therefore less likely to be adjudged disreputable by the school. If the working-class child does find his self-esteem threatened in school, he is more likely to be able to return home and find adequate support there. At school he may feel the sting of invidious comparisons with middle-stratum children and their performances, but at least he usually dresses well enough, behaves reasonably well, and does adequate schoolwork. School may not be pleasant, but its rejection is not overwhelming, and at home he can find alternative behavioral expectations, so that his self-esteem can be bolstered there.

Of course, these differences between typical lower-class and working-class experience in schools and in families are not absolute. Just as the two subcultures merge into each other, so do the experiences of their members, and the boundaries between the two may be impossible to specify precisely.

Peer Orientations and Deviant Behavior

We shall examine here the risks of involvement in deviant behavior during childhood and adolescence as the result of these behavioral orientations but especially of the orientation toward peers, which is by far the most significant for deviant behavior. In Chapter 4 we shall examine the adult consequences of each behavioral orientation. Before we begin, a word on the relationship between age and the development of behavioral orientations is in order. These orientations begin to develop at birth, but the process seriously gets under way when the child enters school. As the child becomes an adolescent, his orientations become better defined and have more serious implications for his behavior. In high school, the adolescent begins to make plans for his future, which is often quite dependent upon what he achieves there. If he is to go on to college, for example, his ability to do so depends upon success in high school. The adolescent develops a growing autonomy—he begins to take responsibility for governing more of his own behavior, and he has more freedom and more time to himself than he did earlier. One might say that adolescence is a stage of development in which the individual seriously begins to exercise his behavioral orientations. Our discussion of the exclusive orientation toward peers, therefore, refers mainly to adolescents, although the problems that produce this orientation have been developing for several years.

Several immediate questions about the adolescent who turns exclusively to his peers to bolster his self-esteem are in order. If a boy is adjudged incompetent and disreputable by the schools and can find no contradictory evidence in his family, what kinds of friends is he likely to choose? What behavior will he exhibit in their company, and how will it be related to his search for self-esteem? How much can self-esteem be enhanced in the company of normatively uncommitted peers? What is the ultimate outcome of such associations in terms of self-esteem, behavior, normative commitments, and life chances? We must begin by exploring specific predictions based on our propositions about self-esteem in Chapter 2.

We can predict, first, that, if the adolescent has been thwarted in his quest for self-esteem in the company of adults the motivation to continue the search in the company of his peers will be strong; second, that commitment to the norms of adult society will be seriously limited; and, third, that ability to secure favorable evaluations from others through social interaction will be impaired. An adolescent wants very much to think well of himself; if he knows that merely doing what adults want him to do will not bring sufficient rewards to enable him to think well of himself, he will not do those things; finally, he will find it difficult to get along well enough with anyone to secure the favorable evaluations he needs. Each of these predictions merits individual attention.

The adolescent will seek others who promise the approval upon which adequate self-esteem can be built, who will tell him he is good, competent, worthy, clean, manly, and desirable. Because no adult provides these evaluations, he is forced to turn to his peers, and he will probably select peers with exactly the same problems. The factors that promote this choice are not difficult to describe. Such peers are likely to be the most accessible, simply because the residential concentration of lower-stratum youth makes them the most numerous and the most visible. They face the same kinds of disorganized and threatening social structures in close physical proximity: They share similar family experiences and attend the same schools. Furthermore, the lower-stratum boy who is severely handicapped in his self-esteem is probably also severely handicapped in his ability to interact with others and consequently less likely to be regarded as significant by age mates who do not suffer the same adjustment problems; youths with conventional commitments are likely to reject, at least over the long run, those who do not share such commitments. The uncommitted lower-stratum boy is also likely to be lumped by conventional society in the same category with other uncommitted lower-stratum boys. Finally, youths with common problems may perceive their similar interests and seek to pursue them in one another's company. For all these reasons, such boys are likely to form associations.

The prediction that such an adolescent's commitment to conventional adult norms will be limited may mean, first, that his behavior may be, for the most part, normative, even though he does not strongly support (or support at all) the norms that conventional society would recognize as underlying his behavior. His behavior is normative either because it is coerced or because he finds the consequences of not behaving normatively too painful. He continues to go to school and to keep on the right side of adults most of the time because to do otherwise would bring unpleasant consequences—punishment from police, courts, parents, and teachers.

In another form of reduced commitment the child accepts the validity of the norms but does not always conform to them, suggesting that the norms have not been internalized and that the absence of strong group supports for normative behavior results in lapses. There is no reason to believe that because someone believes in the rightness of a norm he will invariably obey it, and as we shall see the rationalizations that youths develop for disobeying the norms in which they believe are an important part of delinquent behavioral systems.

Lower-stratum boys with severe difficulties in maintaining

self-esteem almost certainly do not internalize conventional adult norms, and they may even find it difficult to lend verbal assent to them. Under such conditions, powerful group supports are required to keep behavior normative most of the time. Precisely because such group supports are lacking, however, only coercive and situational controls keep behavior normative. The point is not that behavior will be deviant unless externally controlled but that obedience to the norms is a precarious thing. We shall see later that various situational factors often tip the balance in favor of deviant behavior.

Finally, we have suggested that the threatened lower-stratum boy suffers from low ability to carry on successful social interaction, which in operational terms means the choice of significant others from whom favorable evaluations can be secured. The threatened boy typically cannot make others like him, tell him that what he does is right and proper, and assure him of his worth. No matter what he does, he rubs someone the wrong way. And, because he must manage a heavy load of anxiety, he cannot be well disposed toward others. What is behaviorally most significant is that he turns to interaction in which nearly all the participants share the same difficulties with self-esteem and the same interpersonal disabilities, which on various occasions reach critical levels in the group situation, sometimes with explosive results.

Our self-esteem model provides, therefore, the basis for a theory of juvenile delinquency that accounts for some major empirical findings about delinquent behavior. Although it recognizes class differences in delinquency patterns and possible differences in delinquency rates among boys, it is also, as we shall see, capable of extension to middle-stratum juvenile delinquency. We turn now to the theory itself, the evidence that supports it, and its relation to other theories of delinquent conduct among lower-stratum youths.

A Theory of Juvenile Delinquency

The term "juvenile delinquency" does not designate a homogeneous set of behavior patterns that all observers agree are deviant. Juvenile delinquency is not a theoretical category in sociology. Rather, it is socially defined, although social definitions of delinquency vary considerably.[29] On one hand, police and courts enforce and interpret federal, state, and local laws that define the status of a "juvenile," specify forms of behavior that are prohibited, and prescribe punitive or rehabilitative measures. The laws themselves and the interpretations given them, however, cover a wide range of possibilities. Laws governing homocide, for example, are likely to be quite specific regarding evidence, trial, and sanctions, and they are likely to define appropriate procedures for dealing with juveniles who commit homocide. But state and local governments also may have very broad legislation that gives police and courts considerable latitude in defining a youth as "delinquent," in considering evidence bearing on the charge, and in disposing of the case. On the other hand, the label "juvenile delinquent" is frequently applied to both boys and girls whose behavior is loud, boisterous, and disturbing to adults but which does not violate any laws. Frequently, in fact, laws against "juvenile delinquency" are applied to such youths, even though no serious criminal violations take place.

A discussion of juvenile delinquency is, therefore, somewhat difficult because of the imprecision of the term's definition. A youth labeled a delinquent may have committed a serious criminal offense and yet be distinguished only by virtue of his age from any other offender, or he simply may have created a minor disturbance that prompted a citizen to complain to the police. Between these two extremes are many different types of delinquent conduct that vary in the frequency with which they are carried out, the kinds of norms they violate, and the seriousness with which they are regarded.

Some delinquency involves the active and constant participation of juveniles, whereas a more common variety is episodic rather than continuous. Some delinquency involves crimes against property (such as theft or vandalism); other types of delinquency involve crimes against persons (such as assault); others have only participants and no victims (such as homosexual offenses). Some of these forms of delinquency are regarded as serious (such as crimes against persons or property), and others are taken more lightly (such as minor forms of vandalism that are regarded as childish pranks).

Attempts have been made by some investigators to distinguish between *criminal, conflict,* and *retreatist* varieties of delinquent behavior.[30] In *criminal* delinquency the laws violated are often those protecting property, most often through theft. Frequently this form of delinquency occurs in a social milieu in which boys have contact with adult members of criminally oriented subcultures. *Conflict* delinquency involves organized warfare between opposing gangs, which frequently involves the defense of territory and the acquisition of status through valor. *Retreatist* delinquency involves the consumption of drugs as a means of retreat from other forms of juvenile organization and from conventional adult society.

These categories are neither easily applied, nor do they exhaust the range of behavior that is ordinarily called delinquent. Furthermore, crimes often overlap into more than one category. Drug use, for example, often extends into theft and even violence against persons, in the delinquent's attempt to maintain his costly addiction. And, whereas gang warfare and drug use, are serious problems, they are certainly not the most frequent forms of juvenile misconduct today. The bulk of delinquency involves groups of boys (sometimes also girls) who commit a wide variety of violations, but who are neither committed criminals, gang warriors, or retreatists.[31]

In this analysis, we are making assumptions that help cut through the complexities of delinquency by distinguishing between the motives that underlie delinquent conduct and the factors that cause it to be, and to vary. We assume that nearly all delinquents, especially lower-stratum delinquents, share a common set of motives and personal difficulties that are related to the construction of self-esteem. (These motives and difficulties are described at length later in this chapter.) The explanation of the specific forms that delinquency takes—whether, for example, offenses are mainly against property or persons or whether delinquency is a frequent or infrequent activity—must rest upon a number of situational factors. We contend that nearly all delinquents suffer from difficulties in developing self-esteem, from limited commitments to conventional norms, and from difficulties in getting along with other people. We contend also that the transformation of the delinquent's exclusive orientation to peers—in the face of these difficulties and liabilities—into various forms of delinquency must be explained by factors that are external to the delinquent.

Such factors include the kinds of adolescents available in the neighborhood (if there are any other potential delinquents, and if so, what their proclivities are); the presence or absence of adult criminals; the availability of narcotics and an associated network of supply; the degree of neighborhood antagonisms among racial, ethnic, or religious groups; the presence or absence of traditions and values that covertly lend some degree of legitimacy to violating the law; the attitudes and responses of adults, such as parents and police, to juvenile offenses; and historical events and movements that provide opportunities to uncommitted youths for legitimate or illegitimate behavior, such as the Black Power movement. These types of factors determine the content and frequency of delinquent activity, the degree to which youths become committed to subcultural norms that favor delinquency, and the ultimate careers and destinations of delinquent youths.

Many current theories of delinquency posit stratum differences in rates of delinquency. For example, lower-class and working-class boys are believed to be especially likely to violate the law. The existence and magnitude of such differentials have been disputed. It is possible, for example, that the significant differences are between lower-class boys—who we have described as subject to the most severe difficulties and poorest life chances—and all other boys. It has also been maintained that delinquency rates are higher in middle-class groups than police and court statistics reveal. As Walter Reckless has suggested, class or stratum differentials in rates of delinquency may reflect differences in opportunities to escape the attention of the police and courts rather than real differences in the propensity to commit delinquent acts.[32]

Some empirical evidence supports this point of view. James F. Short and F. Ivan Nye found few significant differences between strata in the incidence of delinquent behavior.[33] Their measure of delinquency involvement relied upon the reports of boys and girls about the extent of their violation of a variety of laws, including drug use, driving without a license, skipping school, stealing items of large value, and so forth. Using a scale ranging from 1 (least delinquent) to 15 (most delinquent), they attempted to summarize these violations into a single measure of delinquency. They found that only in their lowest stratum (corresponding roughly with our lower-class) was there any evidence of a link between class and delinquency: 12.0 percent of the least delinquent youths (with scale values from one to seven) were in the lowest stratum, whereas 16.0 percent of the most delinquent youths (with scale values from eight to fifteen) were also in the lowest stratum.

These data appear to confirm the view that the important differences are between lower class and all others and not between lower stratum and middle stratum. However, it is not absolutely certain that Short and Nye's lowest socioeconomic category corresponds completely with our lower-class. Moreover, it is conceivable that a study done on only boys might exhibit a stronger relationship between social class and delinquency, since boys generally have higher rates of delinquency than girls. And, in addition, since this scale measured delinquency in terms of serious violations and much lesser offenses (like school truancy), differences between strata with respect to specific types of offenses may be concealed in the overall rates.

It may be possible to develop a more accurate picture of stratum and class differentials in delinquency if we pay attention to specific kinds of offenses and to the seriousness with which society regards them. The question of the violator's orientation toward the laws is also relevant to the nature of such differentials. There is evidence of striking differences in patterns of delinquent behavior between lower-stratum and middle-stratum youths.

For example, one 1957 study of an urban Tennessee county revealed that *one-fifth* of the offenses engaged in by boys from white-collar backgrounds were classified by the juvenile court as "serious"—including assault with a weapon, armed robbery, grand larceny, and burglary.[34] In contrast, *one-third* of the offenses engaged in by boys with blue-collar backgrounds were classified as "serious." The figures for petty offenses (petit larceny, receiving and concealing stolen property, simple assault, malicious destruction of property, and so on) were *one-third* and *two-fifths* respectively. Serious and petty offenses together thus accounted for slightly more than half the white-collar delinquency rate and for nearly three-fourths the blue-collar rate. There were other differences as well. Truancy offenses accounted for less than 2 percent of the white-collar rate but for nearly 8 percent of the blue-collar rate. Forty-five percent of the total white-collar rate was accounted for by traffic offenses, compared to 20 percent for blue-collar boys. The total rates of offense were 6.2 offenses per 100 white-collar boys in the city and 8.8 offenses per 100 blue-collar boys. Rates of offenses classified by an juvenile court as serious and petty were 3.3 per 100 white-collar boys and 6.4 per 100 blue-collar boys. These data indicate a more serious pattern of delinquency among lower-stratum boys: Their total rates are higher, and their rates of serious offenses are higher.

The data cited in the study conducted by Reiss and Rhodes were gathered from juvenile court records of the names of boys who were enrolled in junior and senior high school in 1957. The rates of offense are thus based on juvenile court statistics and are vulnerable to the charge that the stratum differentials reflect unequal chances within strata to escape the attention of police and courts, rather than unequal propensities to engage in delinquent acts. However, additional data cited by Reiss and Rhodes suggest that the stratum differences do reflect differences in propensities to violate the law. The authors selected a sample of 158 out of the 9,238 boys who were then enrolled in junior or senior high school (all of whom were twelve years old or over). The boys, along with their two closest friends, were interviewed intensively concerning their vocational aspirations and orientations to school, the conforming or deviating behavior of their friends, the amount of time spent with friends, the usual type of delinquent offenses (if any) committed by the boy and his friends, and the kinds of adult supervision provided in leisure situations. Teachers' ratings of the boys were also sought. The authors were able to distinguish between stratum background (blue-collar and white-collar, which correspond to approximately lower-stratum and middle-stratum) and various types of conforming and delinquent orientations of the boys. The following table is derived from their data.

Table 2: Percentage distribution of 158 adolescent boys by social stratum and delinquency orientation. *

STRATUM:	CONFORM- ERS:	CAREER DELIN- QUENTS:	PEER ORIENTED DELIN- QUENTS:	NON- CONFORM- ING ISO- LATES:	TOTALS:
Middle: (white-collar)	35.9%	0.0%	1.3%	0.6%	37.8%
Lower: (blue-collar)	55.8%	1.3%	4.5%	0.6%	62.2%
Totals:	91.7%	1.3%	5.8%	1.2%	100.0%

* Derived from data supplied in Albert J. Reiss, Jr. and Albert L. Rhodes, "The Distribution of Juvenile Delinquency in the Social Class Structure," *American Sociological Review*, 26 (1961), 732.

These data are especially significant because they represent reports made by a sample of all adolescent boys enrolled in school in a community rather than court or police statistics on delinquency. They show delinquency to be more serious and more frequent in the lower stratum than in the middle stratum. Of the 1.3 percent of the sample who could be called career delinquents, all were members of the lower stratum. Of the 5.8 percent of the sample whose delinquent acts (consisting of some petty and some serious offenses committed with their best friends, who were also delinquents), were called peer-oriented, a majority (4.5 percent out of the 5.8 percent) were from the lower stratum. Boys whose nonconforming behavior did not take place in the company of peers were evenly distributed between the two strata. These data tend to indicate that there are stratum differentials in delinquency rates and in types of delinquency involvement, and that such differentials are genuine and do not stem from biases in court statistics.

Such findings can only be tentative, especially since they are based on a small local sample of adolescent boys and not on a large national sample. Some large scale, national data exists and tends to confirm a relationship between social stratum and social class and official delinquency rates, but comparable data are not available for self-reports on delinquency. One very important source of evidence is a body of ecological studies that attempted to correlate the official rates of delinquency in areas within major American cities with social and economic characteristics. While there are some disputes over methods and interpretations, these studies do tend to show that areas of high delinquency are also areas in which indicators of lower-class characteristics are high—such as overcrowded housing, low income, high rates of transiency, large numbers of unrelated individuals, and low levels of education.[35]

The findings should be regarded cautiously, however. Although they do show that delinquency is more serious among lower-stratum boys, they also show significant levels among middle-stratum boys. Middle-stratum delinquency exists, and any theory of delinquency should be able to explain it. We shall attempt to elaborate our self-esteem theory of delinquency in such a way that it can be applied to middle-stratum delinquency. Although the causes of difficulties with self-esteem are different for lower-stratum and middle-stratum boys, we shall argue, the consequences of those difficulties are often similar.

Because juvenile delinquency has been the subject of considerable theorizing we shall precede development of our self-esteem theory with an examination of some other major theories of delinquency. We aim not to disprove them but rather to indicate the points at which they agree and to demonstrate that, when stripped of elements contradicted by logic or empirical evidence (where available), they converge in the direction of a self-esteem theory.

One way of viewing the delinquent activities of youthful gang members is to regard them as a normal, typical part of growing up. Herbert Bloch and A. Niederhoffer[36] argue that, because society frequently tends to block the transition from adolescence to adulthood and fails to provide clear rituals to mark attainment of the latter, adolescent gang activities provide substitute sets of rituals and involvements. Delinquency thus tends to characterize all adolescent groups, and delinquent gangs are structurally similar to other adolescent groups. In terms of this theory, class differences in rates or types of delinquency might be explained by class differences in access to adult status: All adolescent boys strive for adult status, but lower-stratum boys encounter more difficulties in achieving it. But this is not true if access to adult status means getting a job, getting married, and being independent of parents. Because lower-stratum boys are less likely to prolong their education into their twenties, they are likely to marry and have jobs earlier than middle-stratum boys. Even disregarding class and stratum differences, however, the theory is inadequate because it fails to explain why some boys become delinquent and others do not.

One reason for the theory's inability to explain why all boys do not become delinquent is that it pays attention to the formal properties of adulthood—having a job, doing adult work, having adult responsibilities, marrying, having children, and so forth—but not to the social-psychological attributes that characterize adults—the development of motives, cognitive skills and orientations, normative commitments, a more or less stable self-image, and adequate self-esteem. While the prolonged adolescent period characteristic of our society may frustrate all youths in their quest for adult roles, some may be more frustrated than others in the acquisition of these social-psychological attributes. It is important to be able to predict who will be frustrated in this way and who will not. But this theory is very instructive on one count, in that it suggests that the adolescent quest for self-esteem takes on a dimension that was not mentioned earlier: the desire to be accepted on equal terms by significant adults.

In their theory of "delinquency and opportunity," Cloward and Ohlin[37] claim that the motivation of delinquent conduct originates in the disparity between the goals that members of a society are urged to pursue and the limited access to legitimate means for attaining them. When success cannot be attained legitimately, adolescents explore deviant alternatives. The authors pay special attention to the concept of *delinquent subculture*, which is defined as a subculture, "in which certain forms of delinquent activity are essential requirements for the performance of the dominant roles supported by the subculture."[38] Three kinds of subculture are described: criminal gangs, conflict gangs, and retreatist gangs. The kind of delinquent subculture that is formed or attracts a boy depends upon the kinds of illegitimate opportunities available to him and upon his ability to meet group requirements and take advantage of them. The development of a criminally oriented subculture, for example, may depend upon the presence of adult criminals, and a boy's membership in such a subculture may depend upon his ability to take advantage of the opportunities it affords him for success and rewards in terms of its norms, which favor criminal activity. If he is not successful, he will turn elsewhere.

Lower-stratum boys, Cloward and Ohlin maintain, are frustrated in seeking success goals; they seek monetary success but wish to remain within the lower-class or working-class subcultures. (Unfortunately, the authors fail to make a distinction between lower class and working class, using the term "lower class" to cover both.) They want the symbols of success that middle-class life offers, but they do not aspire to be middle class themselves. Their frustrations thus stem not from rejection by middle-class people, but from the feeling that they cannot and will not be able to attain the success symbols they want. Because they are or believe that they will be so frustrated, they explore nonconformist alternatives, thereby creating a delinquent subculture in which deviant behavior is regarded as legitimate. Not all lower-stratum boys develop such aspirations, of course; some aspire neither to symbols of, nor to membership in, the middle class, whereas others aspire to both.

There are serious difficulties with this theory. It assumes a highly improbable sequence of events in which frustration in the attainment of success goals *precedes* the development of an orientation toward delinquent norms.[39] In other words, preadolescent and early adolescent boys seriously contemplate adult vocational problems before they become delinquent and perceive that they will be frustrated. But such a conscious and well-informed perspective on the future probably exists very seldom. It is far more plausible that lower-stratum delinquents are discontented with their *present* positions, as they are well aware of their own deprivation relative to the rest of the society. That lower-stratum delinquents may be discontented with themselves and not simply with their position in society is overlooked by the authors. And, although there is no evidence that they do *not* anticipate frustration, there is also no evidence that adolescents *do* in fact adopt success goals, anticipate frustration in their pursuit, and impute legitimacy to means of pursuing these goals that society defines as illegitimate. It is curious that such major assumptions as these, on which this theory heavily depends, have not been more fully researched. In addition, it seems more plausible to base a theory of delinquency on concrete dissatisfactions than to stress anticipated frustrations. Moreover, as we shall see later, the role of rationalization in delinquency is powerful and it is possible that many delinquents learn, following their delinquent involvements, that such a claim of frustrated aspirations may be accepted by some as a defense of their conduct.

Aside from these questions, Cloward and Ohlin's theory suffers from a remarkably uncritical use of the concept of delinquent subculture. The error is shared by Albert Cohen, and we shall take it up after we have examined his theory of delinquency.

Cohen[40] views the development of delinquent subcultures with explicit delinquent norms as the social fact to be explained, but his account of the manner in which they are generated differs considerably from that of Cloward and Ohlin. The lower-stratum boy is confronted, in public schools and elsewhere in the middle-stratum world, by emphases on middle-stratum values to which he cannot subscribe. These values include ambition, responsibility, occupational and intellectual skills, deferred gratification, rationality, specific manners and appearance, control of aggression, constructive use of leisure time, and respect for property.[41] The lower-stratum child has very likely not been equipped by his previous socialization to meet most of these standards, and he tends to be devalued by the school authorities because he cannot live up to them. Devaluations are especially serious if the lower-status boy begins to *believe* them. His self-esteem is thus threatened, and his search for support leads to the formation of a delinquent subculture in which conventional society's criteria of evaluation are replaced by delinquent criteria in terms of which lower-stratum boys can construct self-esteem. Frustrations need not be anticipated; they are real and present, and the delinquent subculture—a mass reaction formation to middle-stratum culture—is the solution. Members of the subculture approve one another's delinquent behavior, thus strengthening both subculture and individual self-esteem.

Cohen's theory closely resembles our self-esteem approach, in that it recognizes real and present threats and frustrations, but it is not without flaws. The most important—and it is shared by Cloward and Ohlin's theory—is careless use of the concept of the delinquent subculture. The main difficulty lies in the assumption that delinquents define their misdeeds as *right* and that they see their behavior in relation to a set of delinquent norms opposed to conventional, or middle-class, culture. Both theories share the belief, for example, that boys steal cars because they come to believe that it is right to steal and because they are uniformly and positively rewarded by their peers for doing so. The higher the participation in theft, they assume, the higher the status within the group; if status and self-esteem cannot be attained in conventional ways, boys will create a set of norms opposed to those of conventional adult society and will grant one another status in accordance with them.

On the question of the extent to which a subculture of delinquency is opposed to conventional culture, recent evidence suggests that there is a higher level of attachment to conventional middle-class values on the part of delinquents than the theory of a delinquent subculture would lead one to expect. In a recent, detailed study of the values of 163 blacks and 58 whites in a major northern city, boys were categorized by types of behavioral orientations: gang members, lower-stratum nongang boys, and middle-stratum nongang boys. These groups responded to salient images of middle-class life styles equally favorably. The investigators concluded that acceptance of middle-class prescriptive norms is quite widespread, but that the force of middle-class proscriptive norms declines with social stratum.[42] In their large-scale research project in gang behavior, James F. Short and Fred L. Strodtbeck concluded that

> disadvantaged youngsters do not become alienated from the goals of the larger society, that even the gang ethic is not one of "reaction formation" *against* widely held conceptions of the good life.[43]

There is, to be sure, alienation from the adult incumbents of legitimate roles, but not from the broader values of the society.

Of course, it is quite possible that delinquents can be committed to contradictory norms simultaneously, that they can both support the broad values of the society and act in terms of commitments to delinquent norms. Doubt is cast on this interpretation, however, by the finding that delinquents do not seem to refer to such delinquent commitments. Matza, for example, found that on the basis of questions put to gang members (in a social science interview situation, rather than one of official interrogation) about their disapproval or approval of various offenses, most were not normatively committed to the offenses, but expressed sentiments ranging from mild disapproval to indignation.

David Matza has suggested two very good reasons why the subculture of delinquency cannot be opposed to conventional culture: First, the specific content of conventional culture is neither as clear nor as homogeneous (nor, perhaps, even as conventional) as supposed; the most uniform aspect of it is its adherents' conviction that lower-class people cannot or will not abide by its middle-class norms. Second, the subculture of delinquency is made up of children, and that alone makes it highly unlikely that a genuinely *normative* subculture could be formed. "Children," Matza writes, "have a curious way of being influenced by the society of elders, which frequently includes parents, almost all of whom, whatever their own proclivities, are united in their denunciation of delinquent deeds."[44] Delinquents are children, and they lack the skills, the resources, and the personal autonomy required to create a normatively based subculture in opposition to the normative commitments and power of conventional adults.

These theoretical considerations, as well as the fact that delinquents do not typically defend the rightness of their conduct, lead to the conclusion that the behavior of delinquents is not closely tied to norms. Delinquents do not "misbehave" because they think it is right to do so. Rather, as Matza has convincingly argued, the subculture of delinquency prescribes circumstances both for committing and for not committing delinquent deeds. "If some precepts that make up the subculture of delinquency grant permission to perform misdeeds under widely available extenuating circumstances and if others grant exemption from the necessity of so behaving under widely available extenuating circumstances, where is the commitment?"[45] The question is rhetorical. It cannot be claimed that delinquents are committed to norms defining their misdeeds as correct if, under some circumstances, they believe that they are justified in *violating* the law and under others they believe that they are justified in *not violating* the law.

The precepts that make up the subculture of delinquency do not call upon the delinquent to violate laws whenever he can. On the contrary, they inform him of the conditions under which violations of the law can be easily rationalized (for example, when he is attacked or insulted) and under which he can rationalize not violating the law (for example, when violation would jeopardize his peers). What appears to be central in the behavior of delinquents, then, is not a set of precepts that encourage delinquency but rather a common life experience and common problems of adjustment that frequently lead them into situations in which the law is violated. In response to these situations, delinquents rationalize and justify their behavior.

Gresham M. Sykes and Matza call this system of rationalizations, which specify the conditions under which it is acceptable to violate norms, "techniques of neutralization."[46] The delinquent interprets extenuating circumstances that are strikingly similar to those found acceptable by the law itself—except that he interprets them more loosely and to his own advantage. The delinquent's explanation of his own behavior is not an avowal of its rightness but rather an attempt to neutralize the violated legal norms by calling upon extenuating circumstances. Delinquents do not say, "I was right to injure someone"; they say, "I was provoked, and I was right to fight back under provocation." The delinquent's own interpretation of his behavior does not suggest that he believes it to be desirable; it reflects instead a set of cultural precepts that function to excuse violations of the law.

Two facts of delinquency support our interpretation, as well as that of Matza. First, delinquents do not, as a rule, engage in delinquencies at every opportunity unless they are members of an adult-controlled criminal subculture. Delinquent behavior is usually sporadic, precipitated by particular conditions. If adolescents were genuinely committed to delinquent norms, their delinquencies would be more frequent and more regular. Second, the common pattern of maturation tends to confirm the absence of commitment to delinquent norms. Most youthful delinquents do not become committed adult criminals but withdraw voluntarily from delinquent involvements by their early twenties. That such reform usually comes without active intervention or treatment suggests that it accompanies natural maturation processes. If normative commitments were developed by delinquents, it would be reasonable to suppose that they would become more, rather than less, powerful with maturity. That they do not suggests that the subculture of delinquency is not a successful solution to the problems of delinquent boys. This point will be taken up in greater detail later.

The self-esteem theory is consistent with the other theories that we have discussed on many important points. It accommodates adolescent striving for adulthood in terms of striving for self-esteem. It allows for frustration and deprivation as elements contributing to problems of managing self-esteem but not as the sole motivating factors. It incorporates several of Matza's observations on the absence of commitment to delinquent norms, the likelihood that age makes it impossible for the young to form oppositional subcultures, and the strategic import of maturation and the episodic character of delinquency.

On other points the self-esteem theory disagrees with these other theories. It tends to deny the arguments of Cohen and Cloward and Ohlin that there is a close relationship betweeen the behavior and normative commitments of delinquents or that there can even be a normative subculture of delinquency. It emphasizes the frustrations and deprivations that delinquents experience as threatening to the self rather than to potential social success. It views delinquent behavior as a product of problems of self-esteem and identity and of the situations in which boys find themselves.

With this background we can formulate the major propositions of the self-esteem theory of delinquency, using the major points of agreement with existing theories but avoiding their errors.

Proposition 1. The core membership of delinquent groups

comprises lower-stratum boys who have been unable to find viable supports for self-esteem within any adult-controlled socialization context.

Proposition 2. Delinquents associate almost exclusively with peers who face similar problems, and in one another's company they seek some basis for adequate self-esteem.

Proposition 3. As these boys' self-esteem has been threatened and undermined in adult-controlled socialization contexts they have little commitment to conventional social norms. Some boys behave normatively much of the time, although they do not accept the norms; others accept the norms but often violate them; still others have no attachment to the norms and violate them frequently. The reduction of commitment is, however, neither final nor total for most such boys.

Proposition 4. As both individual and group supports for social norms are weak, there is little to keep the behavior of gang members on the right side of conventional norms, except for dislike of the social consequences of violating them.

Proposition 5. Because the adolescent peer group lacks strong commitments to conventional norms and is poorly integrated into conventional society, it is "free" to construct its own norms, but the likelihood of its doing so is small. Its members have difficulties sustaining social interaction and are circumscribed by adult society and its restrictions. Furthermore, the group situation tends to magnify and intensify, rather than to alleviate, their anxieties about self-esteem.

Proposition 6. Group and individual delinquent behavior tends to be precipitated by specific situational factors rather than by attempts to adhere to norms, and it is therefore episodic.

Proposition 7. In addition to internal group factors such as challenges to a member's masculinity, disagreements over girls, and contests for leadership, that precipitate delinquent episodes, there are such external factors as the activities of other gangs, nondelinquent youth, and adults—including police, adult criminals, social workers, and the general public.

Proposition 8. Because inadequately socialized children can neither design nor commit themselves to delinquent norms, and because delinquent behavior generates unfavorable responses in society, group delinquency does not assuage the anxieties of delinquent boys, except for those who bolster their self-esteem by meeting adult criminal standards of behavior.

Proposition 9. To the extent that the attainment of adulthood (and its attendant autonomy) makes new means of building self-esteem possible, delinquent boys tend as they mature to find new contexts of interaction in which they strengthen self-esteem by conforming to normative expectations.

Although it is beyond the scope of this book to develop an exhaustive summary of evidence, the theory can be made more explicit and its power to explain partially tested by examining it in the light of some empirical studies of delinquency. We begin with Proposition 1. We have already seen some of the disabilities that lower-stratum boys face in public schools. We must turn now to their family experiences, which, we have suggested, impede the development and maintenance of self-esteem.

The notion that the family is important in the etiology of delinquency is not new. There is ample evidence to show the contribution of various family characteristics to the formation of delinquents, although there has been no general theory to account for such influence. Sheldon and Eleanor Glueck, for example, studied 500 institutionalized boys and an equal-sized control group of nondelinquents; their data revealed a relationship between the "adequacy" of the home environment and membership in the delinquent group.[47] The delinquents more often came from families that were geographically mobile, dependent upon relief agencies, broken by divorce or separation, frequently characterized by emotional disturbance, generally hostile to children, and marked by erratic discipline. But the concept of "adequate" family environment is hardly precise enough to serve as explanation. The concept of self-esteem, on the other hand, provides a basis for organizing such findings; all the factors listed are clearly related to development of self-esteem and the conditions under which it can be encouraged or discouraged.

The Gluecks' findings should be treated with some caution, however, first because they deal with differences between institutionalized delinquents and nondelinquents, and there is reason to believe that delinquents from disorganized families are more readily institutionalized than others. Second, while the Gluecks attempted to match delinquents and nondelinquents on a number of variables (age, ethnic origin, intelligence, and socioeconomic conditions of their neighborhoods), there is evidence that they were not entirely successful. While both groups were drawn primarily from the lower stratum, the institutionalized delinquents seem to be somewhat more heavily drawn from the lower class, as opposed to the working class. It may be, therefore, that differences between delinquents and nondelinquents are due to social class differences rather than to family variables, as the author contends. And third, the age distribution of the two groups is, on the whole, younger than is typical of most delinquent populations. A significant number of the delinquents (about one-quarter) first appeared in court under 11 years of age, which may be due to family variables—such as broken homes—that have a more powerful effect in the preadolescent period. As one study shows, boys are more likely to suffer from broken homes before adolescence than during.[48]

"Firm" evidence of the importance of family variables is to be found in a study by F. Ivan Nye,[49] who examined the effects of several kinds of family relationships on juvenile delinquency, relying upon the children's own reports of their behavior as his measure of delinquency. He was interested in the maintenance of social control within the family and in any correlation between breakdown in such control and involvement in delinquency. Nye's findings lend strong support to the proposition that delinquents do not find viable bases for adequate self-esteem within the family. If boys do not find such bases within their families, they tend to reject parents and to be rejected by them, to perceive the punishments inflicted upon them as unfair, and to believe that preference is shown to siblings. They tend to come from families in which punishments are not explained.

On Nye's scale of parent-child acceptance, when father and child are classified as mutually accepting, 87 percent of the children are in the least delinquent group and 13 percent are in the most delinquent group. At the other end of his scale, when father and child are mutually rejecting, 48 percent of the children are in the most delinquent category. At the midpoint of the scale (mutual partial acceptance) 30 percent are in the most delinquent group.[50] To the extent that the acceptance-rejection dimension measures the presence of viable supports for self-esteem within the family, delinquents appear less likely than nondelinquents to have found such supports. Other data from the same study show that 55 percent of those boys who thought that their fathers were seldom or never fair in their punishments were in the most delinquent category, compared to 30 percent of the boys who thought that their fathers were always fair. The same pattern holds for feelings that parents are partial to other siblings.[51] Finally, 40 percent of the children who reported that their fathers seldom or never gave reasons for punishing them were in the most delinquent category, compared to 24 percent of those who reported that their fathers always explained.[52] The clear implication is that delinquents face more obstacles to the development of self-esteem within their families than do nondelinquents.

Nye's data are especially useful because his scale of delinquency (on which "most delinquent" and "least delinquent" are the extreme scalar values) essentially reflects the seriousness of offenses as reported by adolescents themselves. Two factors, however, somewhat reduce the usefulness of his findings for our purposes. First, the data combine lower- and middle-strata. This in itself is not a serious fault, but we have so far discussed only delinquency in the lower stratum. Second, the data combine the responses of both boys and girls, whereas we have explicitly oriented the present theory to boys only, under the assumption that the impact of stratification is different for boys and girls. However, it is also important to point out that girls, who are demonstrably more influenced toward delinquent conduct by broken homes, may also be more sensitive to family variables in general. Nye's findings could, therefore, be somewhat exaggerated, but even considering these problems his analysis is the most convincing yet available.

The literature of sociology, psychology, social work, and psychiatry has been filled with references to the place of the family in the causation of delinquency for the last half-century. Out of this literature, a number of tentative conclusions may be drawn. We shall attempt to list these conclusions here and then to examine their bearing upon the self-esteem theory of delinquency.[53]

First, while there is mixed evidence concerning the effects of homes broken by divorce, separation, desertion, or death on adolescent boys' involvement in delinquency, there is general agreement that broken homes expose all girls and preadolescent boys to greater risks of delinquency. The offenses of girls from broken homes, however, very often involve running away from home or "ungovernability," which seem to be closely related to the difficulty of asserting effective control over the behavior of a girl from such an environment.

Second, there is some agreement that younger and intermediate children (the later with both older and younger siblings) have greater involvement in delinquency than older children.

Third, a number of studies report that juvenile delinquency is related to family solidarity and the marital adjustment of parents. Boys, and sometimes girls, who come from homes marked by marital unhappiness and low family cohesiveness are more likely to be delinquent than those from close homes with happily married parents.

Fourth, a number of studies have shown the independent effect of discipline upon delinquency, in terms of its consistency and perceived fairness. Where discipline is consistent and where youths perceive its application as fair, there is less risk of delinquency. A major problem in these findings is that delinquents and nondelinquents might perceive discipline qualitatively identical in different ways.

Fifth, affection, especially on the part of the father, has been demonstrated to be associated with delinquency—the less affectionate the family setting, the greater the risk of delinquency.

The significant point of these findings is the variables that relate to delinquency are also the variables we have linked to the development of self-esteem. (The one real exception is birth order and self-esteem: Rosenberg and Coopersmith agree that only children are more likely to have high self-esteem, but whether it is a disadvantage to be a younger or intermediate child is not clear, although Coopersmith did find that a majority of the boys who had low self-esteem were either younger or intermediate children.) Such correspondences do not, in any sense, constitute "proof" of our theory, although they do suggest that our theory is on the right track.

It is not generally disputed that delinquency emerges mainly when members of juvenile groups search for solutions to their problems in one another's company. At issue, however, is the nature of the problems faced by delinquents and their ability to find solutions in the group situation. A number of lines of argument and evidence encourage the view that self-esteem is a primary motivation in the delinquent group and that no solutions to problems of self-esteem are provided there.

One line of evidence involves the extent to which delinquents are committed to conventional norms. The subcultural approach to delinquency typified by Cohen and others suggests that the delinquent rejects conventional norms in favor of deviant alternatives. Yet, as we have indicated previously, other scholars have concluded that conventional norms are not so clearly rejected. There is also recent evidence that delinquents do not claim normative support for their behavior. Richard A. Ball[54] attempted to measure the kinds of responses given by delinquents in relation to their behavior by first developing descriptions of ten specific situations of delinquency—each involving the commission of an offense of a specific type and degree of severity by a sixteen-year-old boy—and then asking a sample of college students to rank these situations of delinquency according to seriousness as they thought their mothers would rank them. Ball then prepared an average of eighty items that represented a potential excuse for the behavior described in the situation for each situation. "Judges" (professional sociologists) were then asked to rate each item in terms of the degree to which they felt it reflected a "technique of neutralization," which is a response to deviance that does not morally defend the behavior but excuses it by asserting that norms or laws proscribing the behavior do not apply because of extenuating circumstances. For example, if the delinquent is condemned for an offense, he may reply that no harm was really done to his victim. Only those items rated by the judges as definitely indicative of neutralization techniques were ultimately used. Finally, four situations were used in the collection of data, with ten items that were indicative of a technique of neutralization associated with each situation. Two samples of adolescent boys—one from an ordinary high school and one from an institution for male delinquents—were selected, and each boy was asked to reflect on the situations and indicate which responses (techniques of neutralization) he thought were acceptable as defenses for the behavior. The delinquent sample accepted more items than the high school sample. And, when a self-reporting scale of delinquency was administered to the two samples combined and the boys were classified as "more seriously" and "less seriously" delinquent, the more seriously delinquent boys tended to accept more of the techniques of neutralization. Thus, it appears that there is direct evidence concerning the attitudes of delinquents toward their own behavior. This evidence along with the evidence that delinquents do not really reject conventional norms leads one to believe that delinquent behavior does not provide the normatively satisfying solution to the problems of delinquents that the subcultural theorists believe it does.

In another approach predictions about the peer-group experience are based on propositions about self-esteem. The goal of each individual member of the group is to bolster and maintain his own self-esteem. For the group as a whole there are no powerful conventional norms in terms of which individuals can pursue their own goals. The hypothesis favored by proponents of the subcultural theory is that new norms are created to serve as the basis for self-esteem and subcultural loyalties. We suggest, however, that no new norms are generated; instead what develops may be called a "system of shared misunderstandings."[55]

Adolescents are probably incapable of forming independent subcultures. They are hemmed in by conventional society and are relatively powerless to prevent official representatives of that society from intervening in their affairs. The delinquent subculture is not isolated from the rest of society; it is integrated because adolescents are surrounded by conventional adults who have authority over them. Furthermore, creation of an oppositional subculture requires a more complete rejection of conventional norms than the evidence suggests exists. Indeed, even if delinquents did totally reject conventional norms, it is doubtful that they could replace them with norms of their own. That they are relatively uncommitted to conventional norms is a clue to their poor socialization in role skills and internalized behavior controls requisite to the formation of group norms.

It does not appear plausible, therefore, that relatively un-socialized children can or do create the subcultural norms required to sustain their loyalties and to solve their problems in the manner described by the subcultural theorists. We have suggested some of the factors that account for this implausibility. In addition, as Matza has shown, delinquents do not righteously avow the morality of their behavior; in fact, they register disapproval.[56] We have cited evidence that they continue to support at least some conventional norms. Finally, there is evidence that, although peers may exert powerful situational pressures on one another, concepts of rightness rarely follow from experiences with peers.[57]

What is crucial, however, is that each delinquent *believes* that others are committed to their behavior, even though he knows that he himself is not. Matza has argued this point elegantly:

> An ideology of delinquency in the sense of a coherent viewpoint is implicit in delinquent action, but this ideology is not known to delinquents. They are not conscious of an ideology because they have not bothered to work it out. Thus, they infer ideology from each other. . . . The mutual inference is a delinquent subculture. Each member believes that others are committed to their delinquencies. But what about each member, what does he believe of himself? Has he not revealed in a variety of other situations that he is not so committed? Possibly, he is transformed in the situation of company to a committed delinquent by dint of the cues he has received from others. Possibly, however, each member believes himself to be an exception in the company of committed delinquents. The intricate system of cues may be miscues. Since the subculture must be construed from the situation of company, it may be misconstrued.[58]

This system of erroneous beliefs is based on isolation, and this individual isolation results from the delinquent's anxieties about himself.

Members of delinquent groups suffer incessantly from anxieties about how they stand as members of the group and from anxieties about their masculinity; both kinds of anxiety are symptomatic of more fundamental, pervasive anxiety about the self. The intensity of such anxieties is measured by the frequent practice of *sounding*, or challenging the worth and masculinity of other members of the group. Sounding others reflects one's own anxieties, and, though it may temporarily relieve such anxieties, in the end they are intensified. He who challenges is also challenged, and thus the derogation of others does nothing to improve self-esteem. In the company of peers the only real defense against more anxiety is the maintenance of isolation, but in concealing anxiety about self the delinquent boy also conceals his doubts about his own conduct. The system of shared misunderstandings is thus perpetuated by the private anxieties of delinquents, who in talking to one another fail to communicate their uncertainties and so mislead and misunderstand one another.

Why does law-violating behavior take place in the company of peers? The answer must be sought in the nature and setting of the struggle for self-esteem within the peer group. There are two sources of continuing frustration of the delinquent's wishes and needs that help to provide an answer: the community of conventional adults and the delinquent peer group itself.

The intervention of the middle-stratum directors of the conventional society does not cease when the lower-status boy affiliates himself with a peer group. Even his innocent activities in the group often bring the censure of adults, especially of public officials like the police. When he does violate the law (as perhaps most adolescents do at one time or another), he is likely to be treated disrespectfully and thus to have his self-esteem damaged even further. He thus continues to be devalued and frustrated by conventional society, and when frustration impels him to aggressive behavior it is likely to take place in the company of peers who are also frustrated. Although the youth may not be fully alienated from conventional norms, he is unfavorably disposed toward adults and is thus likely to view them, at least from time to time, as legitimate targets of aggression.[59]

The peer group itself provides frustrations because of the public way in which the search for self-esteem must be carried on, because of the intense need to shield one's own anxieties, and because of the tendency of peers to arouse one another's anxieties. One consequence of the frustrating peer-group situation is aggression, which may be directed toward one's peers but is more likely to be displaced upon conventional society or upon other adolescent groups.

Whatever the causes, aggressive, law-violating behavior, is usually episodic. Without commitment to delinquent norms there are no positive motivations to violate laws and good reasons to avoid it. Under some conditions, however, law-violating behavior occurs in response to the demands of particular situations. Attacks upon one's person or self-esteem by other juveniles, challenges to masculine integrity that must be answered, the special hostility of police and other adults, threats by other delinquent groups, and similar events tend to precipitate episodes of delinquent behavior in which the risks are momentarily forgotten. These episodes may involve conflict within or between groups of adolescents; crimes against other people; the theft of cars and group joyrides; disturbing the peace of conventional adults without committing serious offenses; the use of drugs or alcohol; deviant heterosexual or homosexual behavior; and countless other forms of behavior that society regards as undesirable. The use of the term precipitate is deliberate: The delinquent-gang situation is potentially explosive at all times, and sometimes little is required to set it off. The problems of delinquents are aggravated by the construction of so many acts as violations of the law: fighting, using offensive language, stealing cars, stealing other property, being a nuisance to adults, staying out of school, carrying weapons, loitering, violating curfews, and the like. Some instances of juvenile behavior are quite simply illegal; others are ambiguous, and their definition as illegal tends to increase the areas of potentially self-destructive behavior, making it easier for society to define boys as serious deviants.

When they violate laws, delinquents must face the responses of conventional authorities and the meanings of their own actions. It is in the process of explanation and rationalization, to themselves and others, that delinquents convince one another— but not themselves—that they are committed to their behavior. Each delinquent episode and the response it brings from authorities contribute to the belief that other peers believe delinquent actions are justified. Each episode calls forth an explanation in the form of a defensive rationalization, and each explanation is a further miscue in the system of miscues sustained by the private anxieties and public bravado of delinquent boys.

The delinquent peer group provides only unsatisfactory solutions to its members' problems. Self-esteem is seldom found in this context because there are few or no norms governing conduct for which favorable evaluations can be received and translated into self-esteem. How can self-esteem be based upon behavior that, even though it may win applause from peers, can not be defended in terms of rightness but only rationalized? How much self-esteem can be garnered in the company of peers whose own quests for self-esteem lead them to engage incessantly in the derogation of others? Although the motive underlying the juvenile's attachment to peers may be his quest for self-esteem, it is apparent that the peer group is the least likely place in which to find what he wants.

This conclusion is strongly supported by the observation that the young do not for the most part continue their juvenile delinquency as adult criminals. Reasonable propositions about human behavior would lead us to expect that, if commitments to genuinely delinquent norms were formed and were successful in solving delinquents' problems, then delinquents would continue to conform to such norms and would become adult criminals. As most do not become adult criminals, we must be able to explain why. A partial explanation is to be found in the unsatisfactory nature of the delinquent experience, but there is more to it than that.

The voluntary self-reform of about two-thirds of all delinquents by the age of twenty suggests that there is a positive inducement to reform, one related to maturity. Increasing age brings changes in the legal status of the boy; in the way that society defines him, his rights, and his obligations; and in the activities open to him. Maturity makes it possible for the delinquent to participate in contexts of social interaction of his own choosing, and by doing so to create *for himself* means of securing adequate self-esteem. In other words, jobs and girls provide what peers cannot: money, satisfaction and recognition based on work, and interpersonal relationships in which intimacy and rewarding interaction replace challenge and anxiety. As juveniles discover new capabilities they find them more rewarding than gang activities, and they alter their behavioral orientations, cease delinquent behavior, and begin to recover commitment to the conventional norms of lower-stratum society.

Some delinquents, of course, do not reform, and there are four possible reasons for such failure. First, some delinquents have more exposure than others to the adult criminal world and its socializing influences. The more contacts a boy has with adult criminals and the more successfully he meets their expectations, the more likely he is to shift his loyalty from the peer group to an adult criminal subculture in which his self-esteem can be based on criminal behavior. Second, when the responses of police, courts, parents, and social workers to delinquent boys are especially severe, they tend to damage self-esteem even further and to encourage complete loss of commitment to conventional norms. The result may be to force the boy to affiliate with adult criminals or at least to prolong his delinquent career. Third, some boys do not survive within conflict- or theft-oriented gangs or within juvenile branches of adult criminal subcultures; they may thus become involved in the routine of the addict, which involves gainful criminal activity to support the drug habit. This pattern of delinquency is an extraordinarily difficult one to disrupt. Fourth, some juveniles have been socialized almost exclusively by adult criminals and are assimilated into an adult criminal subculture in the same way that most people are assimilated into conventional society.

Other Orientations

Our discussion, which has primarily concerned male juvenile delinquency in the lower stratum, has neglected the role of girls in delinquency and the delinquent involvements of subculturally and mobility-oriented boys.

It is generally agreed that girls are less likely to be officially judged delinquent, and that the offenses they do commit differ from those of boys. The ratio of boys to girls appearing before juvenile courts is on the order of five to one. Whereas boys tend to be arrested for offenses such as stealing, assault, or simply mischief, girls tend to be dealt with by the courts for running away from home and, most often, for problems relating to sexual behavior.[60]

How can such sex differences in rates and types of delinquent behavior be explained? To a limited extent, it might be argued that the differences are artificial. If girls become attached to delinquent peer groups, for example, they may frequently violate sexual norms of the larger society but only rarely be apprehended for doing so. Such an interpretation is supported by the fact that girls tend to be referred to juvenile courts by parents, schools, and social work agencies, rather than by police: Their delinquencies are such that they are noticed only by those with close, intimate contacts.[61]

But this approach does not very adequately account for differences in types of delinquency. Boys and girls may violate norms at about the same rate, but they are different norms. One explanation for the lesser involvement of girls in the delinquencies that typify boys is that girls do not find it difficult to develop self-images that emphasize their future adult roles. School is less important for girls' future roles as mothers and wives than it is for boys' futures. And girls tend not to feel so severely the absence of a fully organized family role system. In addition, because girls find it easier to develop self-esteem and conventional normative commitments within the family, they are more likely to develop conventional subcultural orientations, rather than peer orientations.

What of boys who develop the subcultural orientation or even the mobility orientation? Do they face no risk of involvement in delinquency? While no conclusive answer is available, because of a lack of research, it is possible to suggest some tentative conclusions. It is probable that at least some lower-stratum boys who develop the subcultural orientation are drawn into delinquent activities at some time during adolescence. Because they reside in the same residential areas as delinquents and attend the same schools, it would not be surprising to find that some of them get caught up in delinquent peer group activities from time to time. We know, for example, that the chance any boy has of becoming involved in delinquent activity depends in part upon the rate of delinquency in his area of residence: The

higher that rate, the more likely he is to commit an offense—
even if he is middle class.[62] It seems unlikely that many lower-
stratum boys who develop mobility orientations would become
involved in delinquency, even peripherally, since doing so
would injure their chances for mobility by interfering with their
school work and their reputations as achievers. But even if a
mobility-oriented boy were to become involved in delinquent
activities, he, like the subculturally oriented boy, would probably
only be active for a short period of time. There is evidence that
"good boys," even in areas of higher than average delinquency
rates, are insulated from serious delinquency involvements by
self-images of themselves as upright, law-abiding boys.

In one study,[63] for example, questionnaires were administered
to 125 white, sixth-grade boys in the highest delinquency area
of a large, northern city, in an effort to measure proneness to
delinquency, self-concept, and interpersonal relationships in the
family. The boys studied were "good boys," nominated by their
teachers as unlikely ever to experience police or court contacts. The study demonstrated that these boys had self-images
that were obedient and law-abiding in their orientation, that
their families were stable, and that the boys had positive perceptions of family interaction and did not resent close family
supervision. A follow-up study[64] of the same group four years
later showed that of 103 members who could be located, 99
were still in school, and 95 of these were still rated by teachers
as good boys. Only four had had police contacts. Another study
of boys rated as "bad boys,"[65] and a later follow-up of the same
group,[66] confirmed exactly opposite patterns for delinquents,
suggesting that the involvement of subculturally or mobility-
oriented boys in delinquency may be slight, and that such boys
are insulated from such involvement by the nature of their
commitments.

In the next chapter we shall examine briefly the adult lives of
former delinquents. We shall also explore the consequences of
the other behavioral orientations (the mobility orientation and
the stable subcultural orientation) for deviant behavior in the
adult lives of lower-stratum members of the society. The forms
of deviance are many, and the risks are considerable.

Notes

1. Herbert J. Gans, *The Urban Villagers* (New York: Free Press, 1962), Chapter 11.
2. For a useful discussion of subcultures, see J. Milton Yinger, "Contraculture and Subculture," *American Sociological Review,* 25 (1960), 625–635.
3. Gans, *op cit.,* p. 244.
4. See S. M. Miller and Frank Riessman, "The Working-Class Subculture: A New View," *Social Problems,* 9 (1961), 86–97.
5. See Gans, *op. cit.* See also Miller, "The American Lower-Class: A Typological Approach," *Social Research, 31* (1964), 1–22.
6. For summaries of the relationships between social class and social pathology see Harold M. Hodges, Jr., *Social Stratification: Class in America.* (Cambridge, Mass.: Schenkman, 1964), especially Chapters 7–11. Useful summaries of evidence on particular forms of social pathology may be found in Robert K. Merton and Robert A. Nisbet, eds., *Contemporary Social Problems* (rev. ed.; New York: Harcourt, 1966).
7. United States Bureau of Census, *United States Census of Populations: 1960, Subject Reports: Families,* Final Report PC(2)—4a. (Washington, D. C.: U. S. Government Printing Office, 1963.) For data specific to Negroes see Daniel P. Moynihan, *The Negro Family: The Case for National Action* (Washington, D. C.: U. S. Government Printing Office, 1965).
8. Herman Miller, *Trends in the Income of Families and Persons in the United States, 1947–1960,* Technical Paper # 8 (Washington, D. C.: U. S. Department of Commerce, Bureau of Census, 1963), pp. 1–2.
9. David Matza discusses the problems of identifying and counting the poor in his article "Poverty and Disrepute," in Merton and Nisbet, *op. cit.,* pp. 621–644.
10. Morris Rosenberg, *Society and the Adolescent Self-Image* (Princeton, N. J.: Princeton University Press, 1965).
11. *Ibid.,* pp. 39–41.
12. Patricia C. Sexton, *Education and Income* (New York: Viking, 1961), pp. 199–202.
13. For an account of the nature of class differences in socialization, particularly as they have changed over the years, see Urie Bronfenbrenner, "Socialization and Social Class Through Time and Space," in E. E. Maccoby, T. M. Newcomb, and E. L. Hartly, eds., *Readings in Social Psychology* (3rd. ed.; New York: Holt, Rinehart & Winston, 1958), pp. 400–424.
14. Rosenberg, *op. cit.,* pp. 42–48.
15. *Ibid.,* Chapter 5, pp. 85–106.
16. *Ibid.,* Chapter 7, pp. 128–146.

17. Stanley Coopersmith, *The Antecedents of Self-esteem* (San Francisco: W. A. Freeman, 1967).
18. *Ibid.*, pp. 82–84.
19. *Ibid.*, p. 88.
20. *Ibid.*, see Chapters 9–12.
21. Albert K. Cohen, *Delinquent Boys* (New York: Free Press, 1955), p. 110.
22. There is a growing literature in this area. For example, see Basil Bernstein, "Some Sociological Determinants of Perception," *British Journal of Sociology, 9* (1958), 159–174; M. Deutsch, "The Disadvantaged Child and the Learning Process: Some Social, Psychological, and Developmental Considerations," in H. Passow, ed., *Education in Depressed Areas* (New York: Teacher's College Press, 1963), pp. 163–179; Vera P. John and L. Goldstein, "The Social Context of Language Acquisition," *Merrill-Palmer Quarterly, 10* (1964), 265–275; and L. Schatzman and Anselm Strauss, "Social Class and Modes of Communication," *American Journal of Sociology, 60* (1955), 329–338.
23. The literature is vast. Some good essays may be found in A. H. Halsey, Jean Floud, and C. Arnold Anderson, eds., *Education, Economy, and Society: A Reader in the Sociology of Education* (New York: Free Press, 1961). See also Sexton, *op. cit.*; Howard S. Becker, "Social Class Variables in the Teacher-Pupil Relationship," *Journal of Educational Sociology, 25* (1952), 451–465; Anderson, "Social Class in the High School Curriculum," *Teacher's College Record, 59* (1957), 163–171; and W. B. Brookover, "Teachers and the Stratification of American Society," *Harvard Educational Review, 23* (1953), 257–267.
24. Helen H. Davidson and G. Lang, "Children's Perceptions of Teachers' Feelings Toward Them Related to Self-Perception, Scholastic Achievement and Behavior," *Journal of Experimental Education, 29* (1960), 107–118.
25. On these and the following points see Rosenberg, *op. cit.*, pp. 41–48.
26. See Ely Chinoy, *Automobile Workers and the American Dream* (New York: Doubleday, 1955).
27. See the following research articles on upward-mobility aspirations of lower-stratum boys: R. A. Ellis and W. C. Lane, "Structural Supports for Upward Social Mobility," *American Sociological Review, 21* (1956), 743–756; Richard L. Simpson, "Parental Influence, Anticipatory Socialization, and Social Mobility," *American Sociological Review, 27* (1963), 517–522; Russell R. Dynes, A. C. Clarke, and S. Dinitz, "Levels of Occupational Aspiration: Some Apsects of Family Experience as a Variable," *American Sociological Review, 21* (1956), 212–215.
28. On the concept of disreputable poverty see David Matza, "Pov-

erty and Disrepute," in Merton and Nisbet, *op. cit.*, pp. 619–669.

29. For a discussion see R. W. Winslow, ed., *Juvenile Delinquency in a Free Society* (Belmont, Cal.: Dickenson, 1968), pp. 1–8. The book consists of excerpts from the task reports and field surveys, and from the general report of the U. S. President's Commission on Law Enforcement and the Administration of Justice, *The Challenge of Crime in a Free Society* (Washington, D. C.: U. S. Government Printing Office, 1967).

30. For the distinctions among these three see Richard A. Cloward and Lloyd Ohlin, *Delinquency and Opportunity* (New York: Free Press, 1960).

31. See Marshall B. Clinard, *The Sociology of Deviant Behavior* (3rd. ed.; New York: Holt, Rinehart & Winston, 1959), pp. 208–210.

32. Walter C. Reckless, *The Crime Problem* (4th ed.; New York: Appleton, 1967), pp. 109–112.

33. James F. Short and F. Ivan Nye, "Reported Behavior as a Criterion of Deviant Behavior," *Social Problems*, 5 (1957), 207–213.

34. A. J. Reiss and A. L. Rhodes, "The Distribution of Juvenile Delinquency in the Social Class Structure," *American Sociological Review*, 26 (1961), 720–732.

35. See Roland J. Chilton, "Continuity in Delinquency Area Research: A Comparison of Studies for Baltimore, Detroit, and Indianapolis," *American Sociological Review*, 29 (1964), 71–83; and Robert A. Gordon, "Issues in the Ecological Study of Delinquency," *American Sociological Review*, 32 (1967), 927–944.

36. Herbert Bloch and A. Niederhoffer, *The Gang* (New York: Philosophical Press, 1958).

37. Cloward and Ohlin, *op. cit.*

38. *Ibid.*, p. 7.

39. See Jerome Himmelhoch, "Delinquency and Opportunity: An End and a Beginning of Theory," in A. W. Gouldner and S. M. Miller, eds., *Applied Sociology* (New York: Free Press, 1965).

40. Cohen, *op. cit.*

41. *Ibid.*, pp. 88–91.

42. James F. Short, "Gang Delinquency and Anomie," in M. B. Clinard, ed., *Anomie and Deviant Behavior* (New York: Free Press, 1964), p. 117.

43. James F. Short and Fred L. Strodtbeck, *Group Process and Gang Delinquency* (Chicago: University of Chicago Press, 1965), p. 271.

44. Matza, *Delinquency and Drift*, p. 49

45. *Ibid.*, p. 40.

46. See Gresham M. Sykes and David Matza, "Techniques of Neutralization: A Theory of Delinquency," *American Sociological Review*, 22 (1957), 664–670.

47. Sheldon and Eleanor Glueck, *Unraveling Juvenile Delinquency* (New York: Commonwealth Fund, 1950).

48. Jackson Toby, "The Differential Impact of Family Disorganization," *American Sociological Review*, 22 (1957), 505–512.
49. F. Ivan Nye, *Family Relationships and Delinquent Behavior* (New York: Wiley, 1958).
50. *Ibid.*, pp. 75–76.
51. *Ibid.*, pp. 82–83.
52. *Ibid.*, p. 84.
53. See Winslow, *op. cit.*, pp. 46–69.
54. Richard A. Ball, "An Empirical Exploration of Neutralization Theory," in Mark Lefton, James K. Skipper, Jr., and Charles H. McCaqny, eds., *Approaches to Deviance: Theories, Concepts, and Research Findings* (New York: Appleton, 1968), pp. 255–265.
55. Matza, *Delinquency and Drift*, p. 54.
56. *Ibid.*, p. 49.
57. Short, *op. cit.*, p. 117.
58. Matza, *op. cit.*, p. 54.
59. Short and Strodtbeck, *op. cit.*, pp, 275–276. See also Short, R. Rivera, and H. Marshall, "Adult-Adolescent Relations and Gang Delinquency," *Pacific Sociological Review* (Fall, 1964), pp. 59–65.
60. See Albert K. Cohen and James F. Short, Jr., "Juvenile Delinquency," in Merton and Nisbet, *op. cit.*, pp. 93–94; and Winslow, *op. cit.*, p. 4.
61. See Don C. Gibbons and Manzer J. Griswold, "Sex Differences Among Juvenile Court Referrals," *Sociology and Social Research*, 42 (November-December, 1957), 106–110.
62. Reiss and Rhodes, *op. cit.*, pp. 726–729.
63. Walter C. Reckless, S. Dinitz, and E. Murray, "Self-Concept as an Insulator Against Delinquency," *American Sociological Review*, 21 (1956), 744–746.
64. F.R. Scarpitti, Murray, Dinitz, and Reckless, "The 'Good' Boys in a High Delinquency Area: Four Years Later," *American Sociological Review*, 25 (1960), 555–558.
65. Dinitz, Reckless, and B. Kay, "A Self-Gradient Among Potential Delinquents," *Journal of Criminal Law, Criminology, and Police Science*, 49 (1958), p. 231.
66. Dinitz, Scarpitti, and Reckless, "Delinquency Vulnerability: A Cross Group and Longitudinal Analysis," *American Sociological Review*, 27 (1962), 515–517. See also M. Schwartz and S. Tangri, "A Note on Self-Concept as an Insulator Against Delinquency," *American Sociological Review*, 30 (1965), 922–926.

The Adult Consequences of Juvenile Orientations

4

In Chapter 3 we examined the emergence of three behavioral orientations during the socialization of lower-stratum boys and the consequences of one of them—the exclusive orientation to peers—for deviant behavior. We now examine the likelihood that lower-status adults will participate in various kinds of deviant behavior. What kinds of adult lives are led by those who seek to preserve their allegiance to the lower-stratum subcultures, by those who seek to escape from that subculture, and by former juvenile delinquents—and what are the attendant risks of deviant behavior? We shall examine the social roles these adults play, as well as the chances of inadequate performance in those roles, of withdrawal from them, and of eventual substitution of deviant role definitions.

Adult Consequences of the
Subcultural Orientation

Some lower-stratum boys become oriented to either lower-class or working-class styles of life that center on the family and provide sets of social relationships within the subculture. But such orientations guarantee neither the adequacy nor the stability of individual self-esteem, and therefore the risks of deviant behavior do not cease with their development. In order to examine the continuing risks we must again note the differences between lower-class and working-class subcultural orientations.

The working-class youth committed to a working-class life style has a good chance to develop at least adequate self-esteem. It is based upon adherence to subcultural norms and loyalty to the family, which reciprocates with approval for appropriate behavior. But the working-class retreat into the relative security of the family is not without cost; there is an attendant likelihood of deviant behavior in relation to citizenship[1] and low social participation. Working-class members of modern society withdraw to a considerable degree from participation in the role of "citizen." Such withdrawal is "deviant" only from the middle-stratum perspective on the normative obligations that citizenship entails. Participation is not normative from the lower-stratum point of view, and withdrawal is not deviant.

Citizenship is a status that entails rights and obligations. In American society citizenship includes the right and obligation to participate in decisions that affect self and society by voting and other forms of political participation, to take advantage of widely available public services, and to insist upon a minimum set of civil and social rights. One of the most important ways in which the role of citizen is discharged is by participating in voluntary associations: churches, neighborhood associations, fraternal organizations, special-interest groups, ethnic associations, charitable bodies, educational institutions, and the like. Such voluntary associations provide a means for citizens to secure the full rights and to discharge the full obligations of citizenship.

Yet there is considerable class stratification in the organization, control, membership, and ideologies of such associations. Stratification exists, first, because many associations are limited to membership of specific classes. Voluntary associations that draw cross sections of the social-class structure for their membership are rare and usually stratified internally. Second, those associations that tend to dominate the society's concept of citizenship are generally middle-class associations whose programs of action reflect the predominance of middle-class members.

Why? Clearly, power is one explanation. Middle-class people have more power to initiate and control voluntary associations, to disseminate their ideologies, and to pursue their programs of action. At the same time the allocation of prestige within such associations creates barriers to the active participation of lower-stratum people. Prestige bargaining tends to take place in terms of middle-class values, which allow little prestige to lower-stratum people. Membership in many voluntary associations thus carries the risk of negative evaluations and threats to self-esteem for lower-stratum people, especially those who have encountered such threats previously in the middle-class world of the school. Lower-stratum people avoid these threats by avoiding membership and participation and so become fully committed neither to the principles nor to the practices of citizenship. This avoidance extends even to such matters as voting: the lower the stratum group, the lower the voting turnout.[2] To be sure, lower-stratum Americans do not go as far as the "amoral familism" of south Italian peasants,[3] for example, but neither do they accept anything like full participation in the role of citizen. For the working-class American the relative stability of the family as an important social group and its relative success in supporting adequate levels of self-esteem mean that participation in some forms of associations (such as churches and unions) that are specifically working-class is somewhat more likely. But organizational participation is nevertheless sparse.

For many lower-class people barriers to self-esteem raised in childhood do not diminish in adulthood. For substantial numbers of people, even in this wealthy society, employment and economic security are marginal. For lower-class males economic marginality poses a constant threat to self-esteem, as even such minimum requirements of the masculine role as providing for the material well-being of a family can be met only with difficulty. The inability to meet minimum role requirements means that commitment to social norms is constantly in danger, and frequently pressures are so intense as to encourage withdrawal from the performance of family roles. This result is especially likely when welfare systems, which are intended to help solve economic problems, are so constructed that they actually degrade the male and encourage him to withdraw from the family. A vicious cycle is established: Children are socialized in incomplete family structures, and as a result they are not able to participate fully in the society because self-esteem is threatened, normative commitments are reduced, and interactional capabilities are endangered. The resulting reductions in social competence combine with continuing social-class discrimination to render performance of adult roles, both occupational and familial, difficult. The end product is the socialization of new generations in the same unstable and unproductive patterns. Even if the lower-stratum youth avoids extensive involvement in delinquent activities, his chances to build and maintain adequate self-esteem, and thus to avoid deviant behavior, are not good.

Important questions demand our attention. Why are the typical outcomes of lower-stratum social disorganization crime, delinquency, and mental disorder,[4] rather than purposive and active rebellion against the social order? What of the possibility that our discussion is itself biased by the conventional middle-class ideology of prestige—that people from the lower-stratum are entitled to adopt whatever life styles they deem appropriate, including female-dominated families, if that is what they want? These questions are important and deserve comment. It seems appropriate to supply that comment in an analysis of one especially deprived group within American society: lower-class Negroes. Although Negroes face these problems on a more dramatic scale, the analysis is relevant to the experience of other groups as well. It will not be possible, of course, to confine our discussion solely to lower-class Negroes. Just as the focal point of white regard for Negroes has traditionally been race (without much concern for educational, occupational, or other accomplishments), so the focal point of black organization and activity has been race, rather than social classes within it.

Lower-Class Negroes

By any measure of social stratification American Negroes as a group are worst off.[5] A long history of discrimination in employment, housing, civil and social rights, education, and welfare, coupled with contemporary social conditions, guarantees the worst jobs, the poorest chances for employment, the worst education, the worst living conditions, and the lowest prestige the society has to offer to blacks. Color sets a man apart in this country and contributes more than does any position, performance, possession, or other attribute to his devaluation. Reinforcing the effect of color is an economic structure that has had more room for the black female than for the black male and has employed the latter only as a last resort and increasingly not at all.

Furthermore, Negroes have been the chief victims of a welfare system that, as many of its former supporters now recognize, has contributed more to undermining motivation, demoralization, and pauperization than to maintenance of essential services and the stability of Negro life.[6] On one hand, the welfare system offers serious threats to the self-esteem of Negro clients —and of many others who must deal with it—because it tends to undermine the structures that ordinarily support self-esteem, especially the family. Welfare aid to the poor has been administered through a welfare bureaucracy that performs according to its own conceptions of morality. The result is a system of inspections in which the private lives of the poor are regularly scrutinized by welfare agents. When one's behavior is constantly under examination and motivation automatically assumed to be dishonest, one's self-esteem is threatened.

On the other hand, because welfare services are administered by a welfare bureaucracy, the family's capacity to manage its own affairs is not strengthened. Under current welfare practices, families do not have unrestricted rights over the money that they receive. Frequently support levels are so arranged that it is more prudent to live on welfare than to earn one's own way; some men leave home rather than jeopardize welfare payments because of their presence. The welfare system penalizes effort by denying welfare to those who earn additional income.

Daniel Moynihan argues that a combination of history, prejudice, discrimination, contemporary social conditions, and welfare errors have created a growing population of lower-class Negroes who are outside the occupational structure, concentrated in urban ghettos under miserable conditions, and part of unstable, female-dominated families. Two questions arise immediately: What are the effects of such structural problems upon individual self-esteem and lower-class Negro life in general? Is the lower-class black family structure adaptive to its circumstances, a viable subcultural alternative to which Negroes have every right?

Problems of adequate self-esteem are involved in the deterioration of family structure and in the genesis of deviant behavior in several ways. During socialization the self-esteem of Negro males is inadequately supported by an incomplete family structure. During adulthood self-esteem is threatened by unstable and low-stratum employment, by the welfare system, and by the continuing devaluation of color. The result is a vicious cycle of imperfect socialization: Children repeat the same patterns in the families that they themselves subsequently form.

Abraham Kardiner and L. Ovesey's psychoanalytical investigation of twenty-five Negroes is a classic piece of evidence for the relevance of self-esteem to mental illness, especially neurosis. Their subjects were mostly in their twenties or thirties, and were evenly divided between the lower- and middle-strata.[7] They view the personality system as persistently organized around its main adaptation problems; for the Negro adaptation "is oriented toward the discrimination he suffers and the consequences of this discrimination for the self-referential aspects of his social orientation."[8]

According to Kardiner and Ovesey, the low self-esteem with which the lower-class Negro must deal encourages aggression, whose consequences (such as the threat of white violence or even death) are too painful for him to contemplate. As a result, he must deny to himself his low self-esteem and prevent himself from manifesting aggression, especially toward whites.

One way of doing so is to be passive and ingratiating. Inadequate self-confidence, basic mistrust, and the deadening of emotional response are among the consequences of life in a social system in which self-esteem is perpetually low and violently threatened. The degree to which aggressive feelings are denied and to which the Negro's adaptations center completely on low self-esteem depends upon the way in which self-esteem is threatened.

In the United States, the Negro has lived under conditions similar to those of a caste society: There have been laws or pressures against intermarriage or even informal social contacts between blacks and whites, discrimination in jobs and housing, the propensity to excuse or applaud the use of violence against blacks, and the attitude that to be born Negro is to be in an inferior position from which there is no escape. In the southern United States, caste sanctions have been rigid, strictly enforced, and frequently violent. In the North, lines between black and white have been drawn less sharply, with less emphasis upon violence and fewer restrictions against blacks. Bertram Karon studied the effects of variations in the severity of caste sanctions upon personality disturbance.[9] Using measures of personality that call upon subjects to arrange pictures into various configurations (assuming that the subjects would project aspects of their personality into their arrangement of the pictures), Karon compared samples of Northern and Southern Negroes. He found that personality was more severely damaged under the severe caste sanctions of the South, where Negroes more fully exemplified the adaptational scheme described by Kardiner and Ovesey.

Since Karon conducted his study, conditions in both the North and South have changed. The Southern social code has perhaps begun to become less rigid and the lines drawn between blacks and whites by the latter are now less severe. Karon's study is still relevant, however, because it demonstrates that psychological disturbance—as indicated by the denial of aggression and the deadening of affective response—is deeply affected by the social structure and by changes in it. As that structure becomes less oppressive, the Negro will be less psychologically injured by it, self-esteem among Negroes will improve, and aggression will be able to be manifest more openly. Indeed, the possibility should be considered that riots in Northern cities are at least partially related to *improvements* in the psychological conditions of Northern Negroes.

Interpretation of research findings on the incidence and prevalence of various forms of mental disorder among Negroes and other groups is difficult because of disagreement over findings, different techniques of measuring mental disorder, and sampling in some cases of mental patients and in others of the general population. Some studies have thus shown a higher incidence of psychosis among Negroes, and schizophrenia is apparently especially prevalent.[10] Evidence from samples of the general Negro population (rather than from samples of the ill Negro population) shows a greater propensity among Negroes to give "psychotic" responses to tests designed to measure various aspects of personality. In one study Negro males scored significantly higher than white males on the Minnesota Multiphasic Personality Inventory scales relating to psychotic trends.[11]

In addition to these studies, there is recent and specific evidence of both low self-esteem and high risks of mental illness among lower-class Negroes. Seymour Parker and R. J. Kleiner, in a study of mental illness, psychiatric symptoms, and aspirations among the Negro community of Philadelphia,[12] compared a representative sample of the community with a representative sample of its members who had been diagnosed as mentally ill. They found that their lowest socioeconomic group, which is comparable to the lower class as we have defined it, was differentiated from other groups by lower self-esteem and higher rates of mental illness. Those diagnosed as mentally ill had lower self-esteem than community members as a whole and, among members of the general community (the "well" population), those whose interview records show many psychiatric symptoms have lower self-esteem than those with few such symptoms.[13] (Respondents were asked to state the frequency with which they manifested certain psychiatric symptoms, mainly physiological ones, thereby providing an independent measure of illness for both samples, as well as a measure for those who had not been diagnosed professionally as mentally ill.) They also found in their lowest socioeconomic group a distinctively high rate of diagnosed illness and a large number of reported psychiatric symptoms.[14] These findings support rather directly our expectations about the impact of social class (and membership in a devalued racial group) upon mental illness and self-esteem.

To sum up the argument so far, we have seen that throughout childhood and adulthood various elements in the social structure combine to damage the self-esteem of lower-class Negroes, often rendering it inadequate, making low self-esteem a dominant problem of psychological adjustment. When the social structure tolerates violence to the Negro, legal or not, and rigidly prescribes his inferior position (as in a caste system), adaptation to low self-esteem creates severe personality disturbances —manifested in ingratiating behavior, denial of aggression, low self-confidence, passivity, and deadening of affect. When caste sanctions are replaced by *class* sanctions (unstable employment, uncertain male positions in the social structure, permanent devaluation of color, and domination by welfare agencies) the situation becomes more complex—and more volatile. Aggression cannot be as effectively prevented, because social prescription and enforcement of behavior are not as rigid and the threat of violence is not often used. Indeed, the presence in the urban ghetto of large numbers of youths with inadequate self-esteem is one of the conditions likely to precipitate violence. Inadequate self-esteem is a regular feature of lower-class adult life and, combined with discrimination and limited opportunity, it encourages deterioration of family life, especially the withdrawal of men from active participation in the family circle. Family disorganization goes full circle: from inadequate support for self-esteem and low social commitment, to anxiety, inadequate normative and instrumental socialization, and involvement in delinquency among family members, to serious disabilities in taking advantage of the few opportunities available and further breakdowns in the family structure itself.

This analysis is, however, controversial.[15] Some critics would argue that the conception of adequate family structure on which it is based is biased toward middle-class norms and values. They insist that the female-dominated, lower-class Negro family is highly adaptive to its situation—that, under the conditions of Negro life, it is the most positive adaptation one could expect. Some critics also argue that the analysis of family structure presented in the Moynihan report understates the cultural richness of lower-class Negro life.

The lower-class Negro family structure *is* adaptive to its situation but only up to a point. It serves as a survival mechanism in a milieu in which men are systematically isolated from self and society. As a means of survival in an atmosphere of discrimination and oppression, the family does work, we must agree. But as a means of organizing improvements in the life chances of black Americans, especially when the occupational structure is dominated by men, family life centered around women may be less successful than the middle-class style of socialization. This is not to say that women in matriarchal families cannot raise successful sons—for many do—but that they encounter serious difficulties in doing so. To suggest that family disorganization impedes improvements in life chances, or that the matriarchal family impedes them, is not to deny that lower-class Negro life may be a rewarding experience in some ways for some of its participants. However, there is no evidence of normative support for the absence of black men. It is fair to say that, judged in terms of the material deprivations and psychic injury Negroes must endure, their adaptations are "culturally rich." But it would not be fair, since it has not been demonstrated, to say that Negroes prefer them to any alternatives.

One cost of the disorganized family structure is the magnification of occupational disadvantages initiated by white society in the first place. There is abundant evidence that American society has yet to make a really large-scale effort to end occupational discrimination. But failures in socialization within the family make it difficult for many black youths to take advantage even of the opportunities that do exist.

There is no implication here that Negroes should be left to solve their own problems alone; nor can we offer simplistic suggestions that the quality of lower-class Negro life would show a sudden and vast improvement if only men would rejoin their families and women would stop bearing illegitimate children. The point is that the social arrangements under which these Negroes often must live are such that the family as an institution has been corroded and that its corrosion makes eventual solution of the problem of black inequality that much more difficult.

The fervor with which black militance has been accepted in some quarters provides powerful evidence of the strategic importance of self-esteem in the adjustments of black Americans.[16] Nothing demonstrates the centrality of anxieties about self and manhood among Negro men better than the urgency of the boast that black is beautiful. It is apparent that many Negroes feel themselves part of a social revolution in which fundamental changes in the structure of the self are as important as fundamental changes in the structure of society. What is critical for society at this stage is whether self-esteem is to be enhanced fleetingly in the streets through joyous but violent liberation from the old fear and denial of aggression or through incorporation into the economic, political, social, family structures of the larger society.

Earlier in this chapter we asked why the material and psychic deprivations to which lower-stratum, particularly lower-class, members of society are subjected lead to forms of deviant behavior rather than to organized and open rebellion. Perhaps in view of recent urban civil disorders we should revise that question. It is clear why stable members of the working class do not revolt: They are well enough rewarded by it to prefer pursuit of their interests within it rather than against it. But what of lower-class members of the society, especially those who are severely deprived of social rewards? Do they not have good reason for revolt? Indeed, do not the civil disturbances that have marked urban life in recent years constitute revolt? The answers are complex.

Conditions of stable poverty do not ordinarily provide fertile ground for revolt. Revolutions take place either when the lot of men grows worse or when improvement lags behind rising expectations. Both conditions, it appears, have characterized American Negro life in recent years. The material conditions of lower-class Negroes have worsened relative to those of society as a whole, including working-class and middle-class Negroes. At the same time, the complex network of social structure and ideology that has traditionally kept black aggression in check has been destroyed by the civil-rights revolution. What was most revolutionary about the civil-rights movement was not the passage of laws that can further the struggle for equality of condition and opportunity but the revolutionary changes it wrought in black attitudes toward themselves. The long quest for legal equality through nonviolent resistance and dramatization of the black cause, recruitment of substantial white support for an end to racial inequality, the increasing success of Negroes in public life, the northward migration of the last half-century, and the dissemination of the *idea* that Negroes have rights have helped to promote the belief that the Negro American has an alternative to passive acquiescence. A new "climate of opinion," in which Negro self-assertion is possible, has been created. For some, fulfillment has come through participation in organized efforts to obtain full citizenship in society for black Americans. Others can at last release pent-up aggression in sporadic violence. Still others organize rebellion against the social order itself, not alone for the purpose of securing places for blacks but also to work fundamental changes in society as a whole.

The explanation of urban ghetto riots must be sought, however, not only in the social conditions that have liberated black men from their inner bonds and kindled in them new aspirations but also in the incidents that precipitate violence and the forces that lead to its escalation. The dynamics of the situation, as well as of self-esteem and social structure, plays a part in the genesis and course of civil disturbances, but this problem is beyond the scope of this book—and perhaps of current knowledge.

It is clear that, although the riots themselves have not had the characteristics of organized rebellion, black Americans have increasingly come into direct confrontation with white society. It should not seem paradoxical, however, that partial liberation has brought about sharper conflicts or that the movement toward integration has transformed itself into passionate pursuit of black identity through black institutions. It is apparent that black Americans are eager to create and affirm black institutions in black communities through which black self-esteem can be supported and maintained—and that white America cannot satisfy that hunger. In the long run, the creation of black communities, institutions, and power may promote more honest and successful relations between the races and do more to enhance life chances of black Americans than did the older emphasis upon integration, provided that white resistance does not stiffen to the point at which black pride and militance harden irrevocably into revolution. Indeed, it may be necessary to have self-conscious black communities and black identities *before* social integration and accommodation between blacks and whites can be successful.

Our discussion of riots and black militancy is incomplete, however, if we fail to consider the possibility that lower-class Negroes are much less likely than other Negroes to develop a militant orientation. In his national study of beliefs in the black community, Gary T. Marx found that only 14 percent of those in the lower-class had militant orientations, as measured by attitudes toward the pace of integration, relative equality of opportunity for blacks and whites, civil rights demonstrations, and related matters. Although militants are those who are most dissatisfied with their present circumstances and least patient with the pace of efforts designed to improve them, 31 percent of those Marx classified as middle-class (who would be classified as working-class in our terms) and 45 percent of those he classified as upper-class (who would fit into the middle-stratum of American society as a whole) held militant orientations. It appears, then, that those who are most deprived may be the least likely to hold militant attitudes toward their circumstances.[17]

What can we say of the militant orientations of lower-class whites? Are they likely to engage in a militant, and perhaps violent, quest for better life chances? Evidence from the history of the black struggle indicates so far that several elements are necessary for the emergence of a militant social movement: a sense of relative deprivation and a feeling that serious and unjustified inequalities between oneself and others exist. While it is clear that many whites are as deprived on an absolute scale as lower-class Negroes, many of the conditions that might foster a sense of relative deprivation are not present. Poor whites, for example, do not stand out as a visible group in the society as clearly as Negroes do, because they do not have the element of race to set them apart. It may thus be easier for lower-class whites to blame themselves for their troubles or to accept without argument the society's judgment that they, themselves, are to blame because they cannot easily point to a single factor, such as race, and hold it responsible for their condition. Moreover, lower-class whites have not really had the benefit of the same widespread moral indignation about poverty and discrimination as have blacks. There has been more white dissatisfaction with the life conditions of blacks and (before the present trend to make black organizations exclusively black) more white participation in efforts to improve black conditions than there has been white interest in the white lower-class. Thus, due to a degree of isolation from the black movement, a failure to develop strong organizations and bring them to public attention in order to dramatize their cause, and the lack of a powerful sense of relative deprivation, lower-class whites have not on the whole become militant. In addition, the American economy has sustained record high levels of employment during the 1960s, so that even the lives of the lower-class whites have probably been stabilized to some extent.

Adult Consequences of the Mobility Orientation

We attempted to show in Chapter 3 that some lower-stratum boys become oriented to using education to rise out of the lower-stratum subculture. Their eventual acquisition and maintenance of adequate self-esteem thus depends upon successful achievement of upward mobility. Any deviant behavior in which they may engage as adults is likely to arise from mental illness.

Failure to live up to self-imposed expectations simultaneously damages self-esteem and intensifies the longing for it. The maxim that failure deserves renewed effort wears thin, however, when failure is repeated; the individual must then either resign himself to failure and concomitant low self-esteem or make some kind of ideological adjustment. The former alternative reduces ability to sustain adequate interpersonal relationships. An ideological adjustment to failure requires resolution of dissonance between aspirations and accomplishments[18] through adoption of beliefs that make failure bearable—or redefine success and failure—as well as affiliation either with familiar subcultural contexts of interaction or with new contexts where the adjustments can receive the support of significant others. One may adjust to failure, for example, by denying the validity of the success goals previously sought, by seeking the company of those who agree that success is unimportant, or by blaming others for failure—a minority ethnic group, for example—and associating with people who share hostile attitudes toward that group.

Problems may be no less severe for those who are successful in their strivings for upward social mobility. The dilemma of the upwardly mobile person, as Peter M. Blau has pointed out, is that he must choose between the new social relationships that occupational success requires and his accustomed social ties.[19] He feels he must abandon the latter as another means of escaping his former subculture and substitute new attachments with middle-stratum groups in order to solidify his success. One of the dangers he faces is that the transition may be stressful: He must learn new life styles appropriate to the middle class and risk exposing himself to the appraisals of middle-class people who are more experienced in those life styles. Another danger is that the upwardly mobile person will neither be fully accepted into a community of middle-class peers nor be able to sever ties with former groups completely. He will thus retain a marginal status that interferes with adequate interpersonal relationships and undermines self-esteem because his middle-class peers will not give him enough approval, and the approval he receives from his lower-class or working-class subculture—while important—is less meaningful to him because of his desire to escape that subculture. Because of the large amount of upward mobility into the middle class, however, the problem is lessened by the possibility for the upwardly mobile to associate with *one another* and to grant one another prestige.

To the degree that various forms of mental illness result from the stresses of social mobility and especially from inadequate patterns of interpersonal relations, therefore, both successful and unsuccessful attempts at upward social mobility might be found to be associated with higher rates of mental illness. We must examine the concept of mental illness, especially as it may or may not constitute either a form or cause of deviant behavior, to understand why this should be.

We must first make a distinction between the social recognition of either deviant or conforming behavior and the social explanation of that behavior in order to understand mental illness. In American society, people whose behavior violates certain kinds of normative expectations are called mentally ill. This label is explained in primarily medical terms and suggests that the behavior is deviant enough to command special attention. Whatever the problems encountered by those labelled "mentally ill," and whatever specific norms are violated, the underlying assumption made when they are classified mentally ill is that the behavior is the result of some "sickness" of the "mind" and will thus be remedied by medical techniques.

Two very different kinds of mental "disease" are embraced in the conventional concept of mental illness.[20] Organic disorders, in which some identifiable malfunctioning of brain tissue leads to one or more of a large number of symptoms (such as memory impairment, shallow affect, hallucinations, disorientation in space and time, delusions) that manifest themselves in the individual's behavior, and "functional" mental illnesses, which are the type we refer to in this book, and which cannot be attributed to any organic failures of brain tissue but have behavioral symptoms that are frequently almost identical to those of the organic disorders. These functional mental illnesses (or disorders) are divided into five categories: *psychoses*, which involve severe impairments of intellectual functioning, the disintegration of the self, and inability to live normatively and normally in a social setting; *psychosomatic* disorders, which are physiological reactions (such as certain asthmatic conditions, skin diseases, and hypertension) to underlying psychological states; the *psychoneuroses* (or simply *neuroses*), which involve chronic anxiety and social maladjustment, but not to the extreme degree of the psychoses; and both the *personality disorders* and the *transient situational personality disorders*, which embrace an enormous number of lesser (and less clearly understood and classified) personal troubles, such as "inadequate personality" and "emotionally unstable personality," as well as such concrete forms of deviant behavior as alcoholism, drug addiction, and sexual deviation. Transient situational personality disorders, as the name suggests, are forms of disorder that result from temporary conditions of stress; frequently they mimic the symptoms of more serious forms of disorder.

It is clear from this classification that the concept of mental illness can be extended to include practically every form of deviant behavior. Yet, apart from a list of symptoms (which are very often shared by organic and functional disorders), we really do not have adequate understanding of the *nature* of mental illness. The organic diseases present no great problem, since by definition they have a clear organic basis. But the vast residual category of functional disorders seems to have no conceptual unity, other than that they are not organically caused. One possibility is, of course, that there is some underlying set of qualities that unifies the functional disorders, and that those qualities are specific to the psychological states of the individual and can be remedied by medical solutions. Another possibility— one we regard as more likely—is that the underlying unity of the concept of functional mental illness is not based on psychological attributes of the individual but on his ability to adjust and to get along in his social setting. "Adjustment" and "getting along" refer to the ability of the individual to meet his physical and psychological needs by participating in group life. (The term adjustment as used here includes possible mastery of the social or physical setting as well as accommodation to its demands.) In this approach, mental illness becomes a label applied to some, but not all, behavior that reflects the individual's inability to adjust and to get along successfully in his social setting, and to some, but not all, of the individuals in the society who exhibit such behavior. The label signifies a set of beliefs about the nature of the maladjustments that are called "ill," and about the remedies that are called for. In this book, we shall employ various rates of mental illness as measures of social maladjustment, without attempting to answer the question of whether such maladjustments are most effectively explained and dealt with by the medical model of illness and treatment, or whether "mental illness" is more myth than substance.[21]

Why, then, should upward mobility or frustrated aspirations for upward mobility be associated with high rates of mental illness? The simplest explanation is that attempted or successful mobility make adjustment more difficult for the individual than it would be if his aspirations were lower. This is not to argue that adjustment is made impossible, only more difficult. Self-esteem becomes implicated to the degree that the problems of adjustment revolve around securing approval from others for one's success or for one's adjustments to failure. Where such adjustments cannot be made in normatively acceptable ways—where, for example, the person cannot secure approval for himself and for his behavior—there will be high levels of anxiety and problems in sustaining interpersonal relations. The resulting behavior may be quite varied in content. One person, in response to failure to which he cannot adjust satisfactorily, may retreat to the use of alcohol and find his behavior treated as mental illness. Another person may be so anxious and difficult to get along with that he cannot perform important social roles adequately; he may or may not be urged to seek psychiatric advice, and he may or may not be classified by both himself and others as mentally ill.

What is the evidence bearing upon the hypothesized relationship between successful and frustrated mobility aspirations and mental illness? Perhaps we should really ask first about the kinds of evidence we should seek. Since we have decided to view mental illness as a category of behavior that is defined socially in medical terms, we must be certain that any evidence brought to bear on the question of mobility and mental illness defines illness in a clear and consistent manner. This is rarely the case, especially with respect to the use of samples of psychiatric patients. A sample of patients is almost certain to be unrepresentative of the population as a whole, especially with respect to social class, because the availability of treatment as well as attitudes to illness are known to vary by social class.[22] Therefore, any generalizations about the relationships of class and mobility to illness based on samples of those who have been diagnosed by psychiatrists as ill are made less meaningful because one cannot separate the pure effects of class and mobility upon illness from their effects upon access to treatment, willingness to utilize treatment facilities, or attitudes toward mental illness itself. The best evidence for our purposes would be derived from samples drawn from the general population to which standard measures of mental illness were applied. Such data would avoid the difficulties discussed above, but they are available only infrequently. The conclusions we can draw about illness and social class are, therefore, limited.

On the question of the relationship between successful social mobility and mental illness, one study appears to show the opposite of our prediction. In their study of midtown Manhattan, Leo Srole and his associates found that, among those who were not hospitalized for mental illness at the time of the study, downward social mobility was strongly associated with membership in the category of "impaired mental health," whereas upward social mobility was not.[23] To establish categories of mental health and illness, Srole and his colleagues employed a questionnaire pertaining to psychiatric symptoms. On the basis of responses to these questions, psychiatrists rated the mental health of the respondent. Data presented for the sons of fathers with unskilled, blue-collar occupations (a category that probably overlaps our lower-class/working-class distinction somewhat) show that those who have climbed to the ranks of white-collar occupations are less likely to be classified as "impaired" and more likely to be classified as "well." Those who have fallen into the blue-collar category (whose fathers held white-collar positions), however, have the poorest mental health. "Sick–Well Ratios" (the number of people classified by the study as "impaired" per 100 classified as "well") were 200 for those remaining in the unskilled, blue-collar category, 120 for those climbing out of this category into a white-collar occupation, and 240 for sons of white-collar fathers moving into the blue-collar category. The overall Sick–Well Ratio for sons of unskilled, blue-collar fathers was 150.

What does such a finding imply for our theory? One possible implication is that upward mobility is a rewarding experience and that the strains it entails are more than offset by the advantages it confers. But the findings are also compatible with the hypothesis that lower-stratum boys who develop mobility aspirations are, on the whole, marked by more positive mental health than their subculturally- or peer-oriented friends, so that mental health becomes part of the process that brings mobility about. We will not know which interpretation to support (or whether both are partly correct) until longitudinal data on the careers of boys from adolescence into adulthood are available.

Turning to the hypothesized link between mental illness and frustrated mobility aspirations, the evidence is more positive and more conclusive. In an investigation in New Haven, Hollingshead, Ellis, and E. Kirby found that the mentally ill (in both lower and middle strata comparable to ours) exhibited marked disparities between achievement and aspiration in occupation and population.[24] Jerome K. Myers and Bertram H. Roberts also found such disparities in both strata, but held that they were psychologically meaningful only in the middle class.[25] Lawrence E. Hinkle and Harold G. Wolff's study of a large sample of working-class people revealed that those who were most frustrated in their aspirations and who exhibited the greatest disappointment in their actual accomplishments also had the highest incidence of mental illness.[26] Seymour Parker and Robert J. Kleiner report that large discrepancies between aspiration and achievement are correlated with high rates of all diagnostic categories of mental illness.[27] There is evidence, then, of a relationship between frustrated mobility aspirations and mental illness. That the causal relationship moves only from frustrated aspirations to mental illness, however, and not vice versa, has not been demonstrated. Quite possibly mental illness sometimes prevents individuals from attaining their goals, thus acting as a cause of frustration rather than as a consequence. And, almost any mental illness that arises from frustrated aspirations tends to feed back into the relationship and make it more difficult for the person to attain his goals. We must still move, therefore, with extreme caution in the area of social class, mobility, and mental illness.

The one exception to this rule of caution may be the relationship between social class and mental illness as it is considered separate from the issue of social mobility. The Manhattan study, which is especially useful because it employs a sample from the general community (although perhaps not one that represents the United States as a whole), suggests an inverse relationship between social class and mental illness.[28] The ratio of the mentally impaired to the healthy (the Sick–Well Ratio) is particularly high in the lowest social stratum identified in the study, which corresponds roughly to what we have called the "lower class." According to the study only 4.6 percent of the lowest stratum in midtown Manhattan could be considered mentally "well," in contrast to 30 percent in the highest stratum (which corresponds roughly to the upper reaches of what we have called the "middle stratum"); 47.3 percent of their lowest stratum was characterized as "impaired" compared to 12.5 percent of the highest stratum. There were thus 42 impaired people for every 100 well people in the highest stratum, and there were 1,020 impaired people for every 100 well people in the lowest stratum. Even in the next-to-lowest stratum in their study, which partially overlaps the group we refer to as working class, the Sick–Well Ratio is 360. It is striking, at the same time, that the strata that include members of the stable working class show Sick–Well Ratios similar to those of the bulk of the middle strata. These data amply confirm our view that lower-class people suffer severely from their deprivations, whereas working-class people are able to hold their own with respect to middle-class people, at least in rates of mental disorder. The impact of inequality upon behavior in this area is unmistakable.

Adult Consequences of the Peer Orientation

What happens in the adult lives of former juvenile delinquents? What opportunities and liabilities do such people face? The development of a mobility orientation and the actual attainment of mobility seem unlikely for most delinquents because, as they leave school, which they are likely to do fairly early, they leave behind their contacts with the values and means of mobility. Several other adult patterns of adjustment are possible: membership in a subculture of adult criminals, continuation of the pattern of law-violating behavior into adult life, and voluntary reform and acceptance of conventional lower-class or working-class life styles.

Our theory of delinquency has suggested that the most typical result of the delinquent career is the last. As adolescents become

older, those who have been involved in gang delinquency become socially and legally more qualified to construct and participate in contexts of social interaction in which they can find the
favorable evaluations of themselves and their behavior upon
which to base adequate self-esteem. They find jobs, build roman-
tic and sexual relationships, and frequently join the military
service. In these contexts they are likely to be treated as adults,
even as respectable and worthy adults; such treatment provides
a basis for self-esteem. Although former delinquents still face
liabilities arising from previous experiences, they can at least
begin to break out of the vicious cycles that marked their childhood and adolescence. The evidence is that only a minority of
former delinquents become adult criminals; the rest reform.
There is even evidence that maturation is as effective as professional therapeutic intervention in bringing about such reform.

H. Warren Dunham and Mary E. Knauer, for example, studied
500 male delinquents between the ages of 10 and seventeen.[29]
They found that about 30 percent of the boys were arrested as
adults within five years of leaving the jurisdiction of the juvenile court at age eighteen, which suggests a two-thirds rate of
maturational reform. David Matza has estimated that anywhere
between 60 and 85 percent of youthful offenders do not become
adult criminals. Yet, while research designed to evaluate the
effectiveness of treatment programs has been neither as extensive nor as well-designed as research in most other areas of
delinquency, there is some reason for pessimism for the effectiveness of treatment programs. Joan and William McCord, in a
follow-up report on the Cambridge-Somerville Youth Study,
found no significant differences in the later criminal careers of
matched samples of treated and untreated male delinquents.[30]
Boys who were treated for an average of five years did not
differ from untreated boys in committing crimes as adults, the
number of crimes committed, and the age at which they were
arrested as adults. It should be noted, however, that many new
programs are currently under development, and some of these
may well be able to take advantage of the process of maturational reform, by providing delinquents with opportunities to
construct self-esteem.[31] Those delinquents from the lower stratum
who fail to reform, or who develop early associations with adult

criminals and become committed to their norms, become career criminals, among whom the most typical offense is against property.[32]

For the lower-stratum youth delinquency marks a serious interruption in the cycle of socialization, aspiration, and achievement. The chances for social mobility of former delinquents are probably somewhat impaired, and self-esteem may never be fully adequate for many of them. One recent study indicates that children referred to a child guidance clinic for antisocial behavior (who were followed up over a period of thirty years) experienced less mobility relative to their fathers than a group of matched control subjects, due mainly to interruptions in education and difficulties in job adjustment.[33] Although delinquents often cease deviant behavior that involves serious violation of the law, they may as adults still suffer disorganization in their own families and serious mental disorders. Whereas rates of impaired mental health are very high for lower-class people in general, they may be even higher for former delinquents whose childhood experiences have been even more unfavorable than those of typical lower-class people.

Summary

Social inequalities promote several kinds of deviant behavior among lower-status people. Some avoid commitment to the public world of middle-stratum people and to its norms and cling instead to lower- and working-class styles of life. Conditions of life (including family organization, norms, and material standards of living) are sufficient to keep working-class deviance to a minimum, probably not much higher than that of middle-stratum people if we can judge from comparative rates of mental disorder. The major form of working-class "deviant" behavior is avoidance of the role of citizen and devotion to the family circle and its protection. Material deprivation, social disorganization, and public denigration are more severe for members of the lower class, and one of the most dramatic results is a very high ratio of mentally impaired to mentally healthy members of the stratum.

Those whose social origins are in the lower and working classes and who do become committed to middle-class norms are not likely to become deviant in the sense of violating laws, but they run risks of serious mental disorder if they fail to fulfill their aspirations. Successful mobility does not appear to be significantly associated with mental disorder; one hypothesis that may account for this fact is that the benefits to self-esteem that result from success far outweigh the psychic costs of changing reference groups.

Those whose socialization is disrupted so that they develop commitments to no social norms and find self-esteem as adolescents within no adult-controlled context are likely to become involved in patterns of group delinquency. When they reform and re-enter conventional society, they may face higher long-term risks of disorganization, both personal and social, than do other working-class and lower-class people.

Notes

1. For a discussion of the concept of citizenship see T. H. Marshall, *Class, Citizenship and Social Development* (New York: Doubleday, 1964).
2. For an excellent summary of studies, see Harold M. Hodges, *Social Stratification: Class in America* (Cambridge, Mass.: Schenkman, 1964), pp. 103–115. See also Charles R. Wright and Herbert H. Hyman, "Voluntary Association Memberships of American Adults: Evidence from National Sample Surveys," *American Sociological Review*, 23 (1958), 284–294; and Robert W. Hodge, "Social Participation and Social Status," *American Sociological Review*, 33 (1968), 722–740.
3. See Edward Banfield, *The Moral Basis of a Backward Society* (New York: Free press, 1958).
4. For concise and scholarly summaries of the evidence see the first seven chapters of Robert K. Merton and Robert A. Nisbet, eds., *Contemporary Social Problems* (rev. ed.; New York: Harcourt, 1966).
5. An excellent, though controversial, report on the position of black Americans in the system of social inequalities is Daniel P. Moynihan, *The Negro Family: The Case for National Action* (Washington, D. C.: U. S. Department of Labor Office of Policy Planning and Research, 1965). The full text of the report may also be found in a book that examines the controversy surround-

ing it; see Lee Rainwater and William L. Yancey, *The Moynihan Report and the Politics of Controversy* (Cambridge, Mass.: M.I.T. Press, 1967).

6. See David Matza, "Poverty and Disrepute," in Merton and Nisbet, *op. cit.*, pp. 619–669, for a discussion of conditions under which widespread "disreputable poverty" is created.

7. Abraham Kardiner and L. Ovesey, *The Mark of Oppression* (New York: Norton, 1951).

8. *Ibid.*, p. 302.

9. Bertram P. Karon, *The Negro Personality* (New York: Springer, 1958).

10. A general review of recent literature may be found in R. J. Kleiner and S. Parker, "Goal Striving, Social Status and Mental Disorder," *American Sociological Review*, 28 (1963), 189–203. See also Parker and Kleiner, *Mental Illness in the Urban Negro Community* (New York: Free Press, 1966).

11. J. E. Hokanson and G. Galden, "Negro-White Differences on the MMPI," *Journal of Clinical Psychology*, 16 (1960), 32–33.

12. Parker and Kleiner, *Mental Illness in the Urban Negro Community* (New York: Free Press, 1966).

13. *Ibid.*, pp. 168–193.

14. *Ibid.*, pp. 237–266.

15. See Rainwater and Yancey, *op. cit.*

16. See Gary T. Marx, *Protest and Prejudice* (New York: Harper & Row, 1967) for a discussion of *who* supports black power. The data should be regarded cautiously, however, because even recent data may be misleading in a period as volatile as the present.

17. *Ibid.*, pp. 55–70.

18. The theory of cognitive dissonance, which postulates that individuals are motivated to change their perceptions of the world or their behavior when there is dissonance between their expectations (what they want to believe) and their perceptions of reality, is relevant to questions of self-esteem at several points. See Leon Festinger, *A Theory of Cognitive Dissonance* (New York: Harper, 1957).

19. See Peter M. Blau, "Social Mobility and Interpersonal Relations," *American Sociological Review*, 21 (1956), 290–295.

20. My discussion of mental illness follows that of Anthony F. C. Wallace, *Culture and Personality* (New York: Random House, 1964), pp. 164–198.

21. See Thomas S. Szasz, *The Myth of Mental Illness* (New York: Harper, 1961).

22. See August B. Hollingshead and F. Redlich, *Social Class and Mental Illness* (New York: Wiley, 1958); and Charles Kadushin, "Social Class and the Experience of Ill Health," *Sociological Inquiry*, 34 (Winter, 1964), 67–80.

23. Leo Srole *et al.*, *Mental Health in the Metropolis: The Midtown*

Manhattan Study (New York: McGraw Hill, 1962), Chapter 12.

24. Hollingshead, R. Ellis, and E. Kirby, "Social Mobility and Mental Illness," *American Sociological Review, 19* (1954), 577–584.
25. Jerome K. Myers and Bertram H. Roberts, *Family and Class Dynamics in Mental Illness* (New York: Wiley, 1959), pp. 133–137.
26. Lawrence E. Hinkle and Harold G. Wolff, "Health and the Social Environment: Experimental Investigations," in A. H. Leighton, J. A. Clausen, and R. N. Wilson, eds., *Explorations in Social Psychiatry* (New York: Basic Books, 1957), pp. 105–137.
27. Parker, Kleiner, and H. G. Taylor, "Level of Aspiration and Mental Disorder: A Research Proposal," *Annals of the New York Academy of Sciences, 84* (1960), 878–886.
28. Srole, *et al., op. cit.,* p. 230.
29. See H. Warren Dunham and Mary E. Knauer, "The Juvenile Court in Its Relationship to Adult Criminality," *Social Forces, 32* (1953), 290–296.
30. Joan and William McCord, "A Follow-Up Report on the Cambridge-Somerville Youth Study," *The Annals of the American Academy of Political and Social Science, 322* (March, 1959), 89–96.
31. For a discussion of approaches to treatment see Albert K. Cohen and James F. Short, Jr., "Juvenile Delinquency," in Merton and Nisbet, *op. cit.,* pp. 84–135.
32. See Marshall B. Clinard, *The Sociology of Deviant Behavior,* (3rd ed.; New York: Holt, 1968), pp. 256, 269.
33. Lee N. Robins, Harry Gyman, and Patricia O'Neal, "The Interaction of Social Class and Deviant Behavior," *American Sociological Review, 27* (1962), 480–492.

Stratification, Self-Esteem, and Middle-Stratum Americans

5

In this chapter we apply our perspectives on stratification, self-esteem, and deviant behavior to middle-stratum Americans, who support the dominant ideologies of prestige and control the contexts of social interaction in which they are applied. We shall seek to determine the degree to which the process of differential evaluation affects the self-esteem and life styles of those who support and control it.

Our first task is to determine more precisely who the middle-stratum people are. If we recall that the line between lower- and middle-stratum people is defined by the distinction between manual and nonmanual occupations, we are reminded that there are important differences in life styles between these two strata, especially in their conceptions of the family in relation to society as a whole. In order to deal with middle-stratum Americans we must now differentiate them from upper-stratum Americans.

The upper stratum is differentiated from the middle stratum by the exceptional success of its members in a restricted range of nonmanual occupations. It is composed of successful industrialists and businessmen, powerful political leaders and civil-service officials, eminent members of the professions, prominent intellectuals, and so forth. The line between it and the middle stratum is not clear-cut, but depends upon the criteria of success one applies. One could, for example, define the upper stratum *nationally* by applying national criteria of success, power, eminence, and prestige; its membership would then be composed of top-ranking businessmen and industrialists whose activities are national in scope, top federal politicians and civil-service officials, the governors of the largest states, national leaders of the professions, and intellectuals with substantial national reputations and influence. One could also define an upper stratum for any local community, whatever its size, by applying relevant criteria of success on the local scene.

Here, as elsewhere, the question of defining strata is somewhat separate from the question of locating subcultures and classes within them.[1] To define an upper stratum in this way is not to suggest that it is characterized by much homogeneity of life styles, nor that it forms a self-conscious unit of social organization. Within the upper stratum of local communities there may be rather distinctive patterns of behavior, social intercourse, intra-stratum marriage, and educational and political practices. Within the national upper stratum it is doubtful that this much homogeneity can be found, although the "national upper-class" described by E. Digby Baltzell may be an example of a self-conscious, national subculture of upper-stratum people who regard themselves as socially exclusive, attempt to confine marriage within the class, adhere to self-conceptions as "upper-class," and try to maintain distinctive standards of taste and etiquette.[2] The life styles of the members of the upper stratum as a whole (as defined nationally) are marked in general by the comfort and stability made possible by the resources they command, as well as by their ability and willingness to exercise power at various levels in the society.

The accomplishments and life styles of members of the upper stratum provide a standard against which members of the middle stratum judge their own accomplishments and life styles. In nearly every middle-stratum occupation, for example, there is a tendency for individuals to compare their own accomplishments with those of successful members of the occupation. The standards of taste and etiquette of upper-stratum people frequently are emulated by members of the middle stratum. The criteria of prestige employed by members of the middle stratum, which often take as their standard the positions, power, and wealth of the upper stratum, pose no threat to the members of the upper stratum itself. But they may be threatening to middle-stratum people themselves, simply because they are central to their evaluation of self and performance. Our thesis is that middle-stratum Americans develop large amounts of anxiety about status because of the very ideologies of prestige in which they believe—pervasive worry about their positions and attainments relative to those of people with whom they are in competition; it arises because their ideologies generate doubts about the worth of the individual and the validity of his accomplishments under two different conditions.

First, when adherence to an ideology is the *only* available source of self-esteem, those who do not succeed as they think they should find their self-esteem threatened. In the competition for scarce positions, performances, possessions, and attributes, not everyone *can* succeed, so that some will inevitably suffer this form of status anxiety as long as such achievement is the only criterion. Second, the upward mobility of people of lower-stratum origins into the middle stratum generates anxiety, both for the upwardly mobile themselves (who may be well regarded for their occupational attainments but disliked by middle-class people because of their ethnic or family backgrounds) and for existing members of the middle stratum (who may feel threatened by the upwardly mobile, whom they regard as rivals).

Before we begin to discuss the behavioral orientations developed by members of the middle stratum and the risks of deviance they entail, a word on our use of the term "middle class" is in order. A social class—defined in this study as an aggregate of individuals defined by their participation in a more or less common subculture—is a subdivision of a stratum. Within the middle stratum, it is possible to identify several subcultures, and therefore several classes, often called the lower middle class, middle class, and upper middle class.[3] While each has some distinctive features, they share a good many features in common, including the emphasis upon achievement described shortly. Because the various subcultures of the middle stratum do share so many elements in common, we shall refer henceforth to the middle class, meaning by that term the common elements of various middle-stratum subcultures.

Middle-Stratum Behavioral Orientations

There is little doubt that middle-stratum Americans emphasize the importance of achievement and value highly the prestige it brings. There is convincing evidence that middle-stratum parents are more strongly oriented than are lower-stratum parents toward developing high levels of achievement motivation in their children.[4] Analyses of the whole society reveal widespread status anxiety, status striving, prestige bargaining, status symbolism, and prestige-oriented consumption among middle-stratum people.[5]

For the middle-stratum child, perhaps especially the male, who grows up in a society in which the dominant ideologies of prestige emphasize achievement, self-esteem depends mainly upon three factors. First, because his family and his school promote and reward achievement, his self-esteem will be partly determined by the degree to which his achievements meet the expectations of significant others. Because ultimate income and occupational level depend to a great extent upon educational attainment, the standards of achievement imposed on the middle-stratum child predominantly involve school performance.

Second, there may or may not be other criteria of accomplishment than academic ones in terms of which the child may or may not do well. Examples include participation in athletics, membership and participation in social clubs, dating and related social activities, and artistic accomplishment. Such alternative criteria may be closely related to parental aspirations for children, and, not infrequently, they may equal academic criteria in importance. Frequently, however, the standards are genuine alternatives, which allow the construction of adequate self-esteem regardless of academic performance.

Third, whatever the criteria of achievement, the child may

or may not receive assurances of his worth from significant others independently of his behavior related to achievement standards. The child may be reared in an affectively warm environment, in which there are opportunities for social interaction and rewards not conditional upon achievement and in which parents frequently affirm their contentment with the child's best efforts, whatever the results.

Such factors determine the behavioral orientations of middle-stratum children. Three such orientations can be discerned, and they depend upon the standards by which middle-stratum children are evaluated and their performance in terms of those standards.

Achievement Orientation

Middle-stratum youths are nearly always evaluated in terms of their achievements. Some achievement criteria are set by the school and its demands for academic talent; others include participation in social clubs, athletics, artistic activities, youth groups, and even dating. All these latter activities call for certain skills and provide opportunities for their display, although they are not directly related to the academic education. We say that youths are oriented toward achievement, of whatever type, when the approval they seek is to an important degree conditional upon achievement. Academic criteria of achievement are not infrequently, emphasized to the exclusion of all others, and self-esteem then comes to depend solely upon school performance. Failure to fulfill aspirations or to be rewarded for youthful achievements by improvements in adult social status is the major cause of deviant behavior among the achievement-oriented.

The Intrinsic Orientation

For some middle-stratum children, achievement criteria of evaluation are not emphasized to the exclusion of other criteria of evaluation, if at all. Instead the content of the middle-class subculture—manners, sensibilities, and habits—is emphasized; the achievement aspects of the middle-class subculture are played down in favor of other aspects. Self-esteem is created and reinforced in a family setting that regards adherence to the middle-class subculture as important and worthy in itself.

The Peer Orientation

Some middle-stratum youths can find no means of acquiring and maintaining adequate self-esteem within the contexts of family and school. For some the standards of achievement are too high and assurances of worth in the family too infrequent to sustain self-esteem. For others no standards are set and no assurances given. Whatever the source of this orientation (and there are probably many others as well), its characteristics are much the same as those of the peer-group orientation among lower-stratum boys: low commitment to adult norms, anxiety about self, and lowered capacities for social interaction. Although the characteristics are the same, however, they are likely to be less severe and therefore to have less serious consequences.

Some Predictions and Evidence

In order to test the applicability of the self-esteem theory to middle-stratum people, we shall make some predictions about middle-stratum life then test them against relevant evidence. For example, the sons of middle-stratum Americans exhibit higher levels of achievement motivation than do the sons of lower-stratum Americans. Bernard Rosen[6] assigned a sample of high school boys to socioeconomic strata on the basis of their fathers' occupation, education, and area of residence. There were five such strata, of which two (labelled IV and V) correspond roughly to our lower stratum, two (labelled I and II) correspond with our middle stratum (with perhaps some small upper-stratum representation), and one (labelled III) overlaps our lower and middle stata. A measure of achievement motivation was developed by David C. McClelland and his associates in the form of a Thematic Apperception Test, in which subjects are presented with a set of fairly ambiguous pictures in which the activities people are engaged in are not clear from the pictures themselves. Subjects are asked to write stories about the picture, and their stories are scored for the presence of achievement imagery. If, for example, a story describes someone who is happy because he has done something well ("The boy in the picture is happy because he has done well on the exam."), it would be scored as containing achievement imagery. The assumption of the test is that individuals project their own attitudes and motives into the ambiguous situations of the stimulus picture.

Using this measure, Rosen found a relationship between achievement motivation and social class. In his classes IV and V, the percentage of boys with *high* achievement motivation was about 27 as compared to 83 percent in his classes I and II. In another study,[7] using the same testing procedures and the same measure of socioeconomic rank but using a sample of boys (about four years younger, on the average, than those in the previous study) chosen to reflect various ethnic backgrounds, Rosen also found the same relationship. In that study he found that while social class and ethnic affiliation both influence achievement motivation, the effects of social class are more powerful.

The concept of n Ach (a shorthand term for need for achievement or achievement motivation) may be examined in terms of our theory of self-esteem. Achievement motivation has been defined as an enduring disposition "to strive for success in situations where performance is to be evaluated in terms of some standard of excellence."[8] Parental emphasis upon achievement norms, which results in high levels of n Ach when it takes place in combination with warm and positive maternal evaluations of performance, produces individuals in whom self-esteem depends upon achievement.[9] The concept of n Ach thus provides one measure of the extent to which socialization has created a disposition to seek self-esteem by striving to meet standards of excellence.

If the normative commitments of some middle-stratum youths are to achievement goals and if n Ach measures the strength of the disposition to pursue such commitments, then there should be a positive relationship between n Ach and school performance. Rosen found that school performance, as measured by grades, was associated with achievement motivation:[10] Those with high n Ach scores were twice as likely to have average school grades of "B" or above than were those with low n Ach scores. The relationship holds for each social class and for the aggregate. Some caution is necessary in the interpretation of these findings, however, since inherent ability also has an effect upon school grades—especially since grades may not be the most valid measure of performance. If teachers reward effort rather than performance, for example, or if their evaluations of performance are tempered by estimates of the amount of effort students exert, then Rosen's study only shows that students who are motivated to work hard and to exert a lot of effort will get better grades. Another possibility is that teachers award grades on the basis of social class, so that any connection between n Ach and grades is only a byproduct of other associations between social class and grades and social class and n Ach.

The relationships among self-esteem, behavior, and n Ach are mutually reinforcing. As parents emphasize achievement criteria for their sons, they encourage the development of high levels of n Ach. As the sons' high n Ach induces them to perform well in terms of the school's criteria (assuming they have the ability to do so), their performances and the responses of parents and teachers reinforce self-esteem and dispose them to still greater achievement.

What are the adult outcomes of achievement orientation in childhood? To the extent that the orientation encourages and facilitates efforts toward social mobility, we should expect middle-stratum people with high levels of n Ach to be more upwardly mobile than those with low levels. At least some data[11] confirm this expectation, although the statistical relationships are not strong, perhaps because middle-stratum people can attain some social mobility through educational and other means even when their levels of n Ach are not very high and their commitment to achievement norms is not very strong. Success for the lower-stratum person may depend much more upon achievement motivation than it does for the middle-stratum person.

What happens when the high aspirations of middle-stratum people are not fully satisfied? If their orientations toward achievement have been accompanied consistently by feelings of intrinsic worth and value in the middle-stratum subculture, their self-esteem may be maintained anyway. But if powerful achievement orientation has been unaccompanied by such feelings then perceived failure may have serious consequences.

When self-esteem depends upon fulfilling aspirations, failure reduces self-esteem to inadequate levels, resulting in anxiety and, over the long run, reduced capacity to sustain adequate interpersonal relations. We should thus find that middle-stratum people whose aspirations outrun their achievements are especially likely to show patterns of mental disorder, in the same way and for the same reasons as are lower-stratum people whose accomplishments have not kept up with their aspirations.

Evidence to support this prediction is not conclusive, but it does suggest that disparities between aspiration and achievement among middle-stratum people are related to mental disorders. As Robert J. Kleiner and Seymour Parker point out, an apparent relationship between orientation to mobility and mental disorder frequently emerges in *clinical* settings.[12] Abraham Kardiner and L. Ovesey found that striving for achievement was an element in the psychopathology of middle stratum, but not lower stratum Negroes.[13] In a study by A. B. Hollingshead, R. Ellis, and E. Kirby, large disparities between the aspirations and achievements of the mentally ill were found in both the middle and lower strata.[14] Jerome K. Myers and B. H. Roberts reported the same finding, although they argued that the disparities were psychologically meaningful only in middle-stratum patients.[15]

Damage to self-esteem is, of course, not the only causal factor in mental disorder. Clearly, many others are also involved, but we believe that such damage is an important, even the crucial, factor because of its implications for interpersonal relationships. First, the disruption of interpersonal relationships is part of the symptomatology of many mental disorders. Second, and perhaps more important, low self-esteem encourages social isolation, and the resulting hopelessness may have a powerful impact upon the genesis and course of mental disorder.

Those middle-stratum youths and adults who are not strongly achievement-oriented and who receive assurances of their worth independent of achievement criteria are least likely to engage in deviant behavior. They may share middle-stratum values and orientations, including the ideology of prestige, but their support of the ideology is not so exclusively based on personal success that failure leads to serious consequences. Rather, their style of life is one in which only a moderate degree of success is necessary, and their juvenile and adult careers are judged by easier standards, which they are more likely to be able to meet. The risk is of downward social mobility, which in turn is associated with mental disorder: Numerous studies show that downward mobility is related to increased likelihood of mental disorder.[16]

Perhaps the most interesting (and least explored) consequences of stratification and inadequate self-esteem for deviant behavior among middle-stratum people involve youths whose orientations are exclusively toward peers. We shall attempt now to develop a theory of middle-stratum delinquency to parallel the theory of lower-stratum delinquency proposed in Chapter 3.

Middle-Stratum Peer Orientations and Delinquent Behavior

Our analysis proceeds on the assumption that an explanation of delinquency must be equally valid for both middle- and lower-stratum forms. Our approach permits us to postulate the conditions under which middle-stratum boys become exclusively dependent upon their peers, to predict the consequences of this orientation for their behavior, and to examine the social factors that create differences between middle- and lower-stratum delinquents.

Why do some middle-stratum youths become oriented exclusively toward their peers? The answer involves the special difficulties they are likely to have in constructing behavioral logics that link norms and expectations, favorable appraisals, and self-esteem. For some, difficulties may arise because they cannot meet the academic or other standards of achievement imposed upon them by parents and teachers. Others may receive little assurance of their worth in terms of conformity to middle-stratum norms apart from achievement norms. In any case, self-esteem does not develop adequately in the company of and under the direction of significant adults.

Albert K. Cohen has also raised the possibility that recent structural changes in American society have increased the frequency of middle-stratum delinquency.[17] He argues that children of the affluent middle classes do not see as clearly as their parents do the connections betwen current activity and future success. When resources are abundant and school systems promote and reward regardless of achievement, the child who is subject to high achievement expectations may find it difficult to understand why he should devote himself to hard work. In Cohen's view this child turns to the company of his peers because he has plenty of time, because they provide more pleasant company than do adults, and because he is encouraged to do so by adults. Questions of self-esteem may also be implicated in this explanation of peer orientations among middle-stratum children, which Cohen considers to be increasing. If the child can see no intrinsic reason for trying to achieve—if the demands of parents and teachers seem irrelevant—he may cease to try and thus be faced with negative appraisals and eventual loss of self-esteem. The quest for self-esteem may reinforce his tendency to turn to his peers, for the apparent irrelevance of achievement makes parental insistence even more painful: He may feel he is being punished for failing to do unimportant things.

Whatever the causes of his loss of self-esteem, the consequences include reduced commitment to conventional social norms, the need to seek self-esteem within the context of some significant social group, and a large fund of anxiety about self, which makes interpersonal relationships difficult. Several factors lead us to believe that the specific experiences of lower- and middle-stratum delinquents will be quite different, however; we shall try to explore some of the similarities and differences.

The middle-stratum adolescent probably associates with peers for the same reasons that the lower-stratum adolescent does, and he probably chooses middle-stratum adolescents who share his adjustment problems. If such peers are not available to him, he must choose from those who are: other middle-stratum adolescents, lower-stratum nondelinquents (either subculturally or mobility-oriented), and lower-stratum delinquents. It is difficult to predict the order in which selection will take place, although the order in which we have listed the groups seems likely. If the boy chooses nondelinquent lower-stratum peers there is evidence that his own chances for upward social mobility are thereby reduced.[18]

Several kinds of evidence are available: There are lower-stratum gangs and middle-stratum gangs, but there is little evidence of class mixing within gangs. (The word "gang" is used here to denote more or less stable groups of delinquency-prone adolescent boys in general and not just violent gangs engaging in organized warfare, which is a phenomenon that has diminished in frequency and public attention in recent years.) There is evidence that most middle-stratum delinquency is peer-oriented.[19] There is further evidence of an association between ability (as measured by IQ) and delinquency among middle-stratum boys: Boys in low-ability groups show higher rates of serious, petty, and truancy offenses (as classified by courts) than do boys in high-ability groups.[20] There is also evidence that the class structure of the neighborhood and school has an impact upon middle-stratum delinquency rates: In schools with higher proportions of lower-stratum students and in neighborhoods where general delinquency rates are higher, rates are higher even for middle-stratum boys.[21]

What are the characteristics of middle-stratum delinquency? One of the most striking observations arises not from hard empirical evidence but from its absence: There are few data on middle-stratum delinquency, nor do we find long-term public alarm or awareness of it as a social problem. Delinquency has largely been construed as an urban, lower-stratum problem.[22] Apparently, public definitions of the two varieties of delinquency have been different, and the difference may reflect the specific characteristics of middle-stratum delinquents, the nature of their behavior, and the reactions of officials and other involved middle-stratum adults.

The middle-stratum youth is in a more favorable position than is his lower-stratum counterpart even when his self-esteem is seriously threatened. The first element in his favor is that damage to his self-esteem is likely to be less severe than that of the lower-stratum boy. Whereas the latter suffers from very painful negative evaluations, the middle-stratum boy is more likely to experience only the absence of positive evaluations. The middle-stratum boy has probably developed the ability to behave in conventional middle-stratum ways if not the desire to do so. The middle-stratum boy also has access to more resources; cars and money, for example, are readily available legally, and middle-stratum delinquencies frequently reflect this fact.[23] When he does violate the law, the middle-stratum boy may also stand a better chance of concealing it.

This ability to conceal violations partly reflects the resources that are available—parents may quietly pay damages—but it also reflects softer official reactions to middle-stratum delinquency than to lower-stratum delinquency. Middle-stratum parents have access to social and political influence, which frequently results in the nonintervention of the police and which lower-stratum parents do not have. The middle-stratum world also contains a network of social institutions prepared to absorb and care for middle-stratum delinquents. Whereas the lower-stratum delinquent will probably encounter the police and courts and is more likely to be institutionalized, especially if his family is disorganized, the middle-stratum delinquent is in many cases turned over to his parents and in their custody he may have access to private helping agencies.

As a result of such factors the middle-stratum delinquent is less likely to define himself and to be defined by others as a delinquent and a lawbreaker. Whereas lower-stratum delinquency feeds upon official definitions of boys as criminals and lawbreakers, middle-status boys are insulated from such experiences and resulting self-definitions by a subculture that is prepared to allow them "mistakes," some claims to worth in spite of such mistakes, help, and some hope for the future. Although the lower-stratum delinquent constructs (on the basis of such misunderstood legal defenses as the principle that assault committed in the defense of one's property is not a crime), techniques of neutralization that function as excuses for violating laws, the middle-stratum boy finds functional equivalents in sociological and psychiatric explanations of his behavior (which are also frequently misunderstood). He is told, and perhaps comes to believe, that he has problems of adjustment or that he is simply seeking attention; combined with the treatment that follows, such explanations help make his behavior coherent to him and eventually to bring him back into conventional middle-stratum society.

How does existing theory account for juvenile delinquency in the middle classes? Talcott Parsons focused on typical Western patterns of socialization, arguing that both boys and girls form early identifications with their mothers but that during the course of socialization boys come under pressure to assert their masculinity.[24] Such assertion requires a revolt against the mother, because the boy's early and close ties to her have produced a subconscious association between "goodness" and femininity. Masculinity, therefore, comes to be associated with "badness," and being a "bad boy" comes to be a goal, and boyish behavior by definition takes antisocial directions. Cohen[25] has added that middle-stratum boys face special problems in asserting their masculinity because in the process of growing up they see less of their fathers in the performance of occupational roles. This problem is aggravated by the prolonged dependence of the middle-stratum boy upon his parents and the long postponement of a genuine adult masculine role.

The problems of socialization—of asserting adult masculine identities—are more or less common to all youths. Although such problems undoubtedly influence the behavior of all, we must be wary of relying upon them for a full explanation. Because not all boys become delinquent, we cannot explain the behavior of those who do by citing only the experiences common to all. Other, more specific, problems must be involved, and we have attempted to conceptualize them in terms of self-esteem. Furthermore, it is difficult to demonstrate that middle-stratum boys are more mother-dominated than are lower-stratum boys. Lower-class boys, indeed, would face this problem most severely because of the frequent domination of the family by women. Masculinity is to a great extent what is defined by the social group, and in this connection middle-stratum boys apparently have greater resources than lower-stratum boys enabling them to assert masculine self-images: They can conform to conventional norms more easily, they have more material resources, and their deviations from norms are less severely regarded. It may well be that the middle-class boy is able to define dependence upon his parent during his pursuit of secondary and higher education as a normatively appropriate way of acquiring a genuine adult role, whereas the boy from the lower stratum finds this difficult.

We see then that lower- and middle-stratum delinquency can be explained within the same theoretical framework, and the similarities and differences between the two are meaningful in theoretical terms. Both middle-stratum and lower-stratum delinquents face the problems of low self-esteem, and both are engaged in efforts to bolster self-esteem in the company of peers. The middle-stratum boy is, however, less severely threatened, less completely oriented to the peer group, less completely lacking in conventional normative commitments, and less injured in his capacity to sustain social interaction. At the same time, when the middle-stratum youth does violate the law, he meets with less condemnation from his parents and from officials. Although a great deal more research on middle-stratum delinquency is necessary, this extension of the self-esteem theory suggests some of the lines along which such research might proceed.

One area that has yet to receive adequate sociological treatment, for example, is drug use by middle-class adolescents.[26] There has been a marked increase in public attention in recent years given to such drugs as marijuana, LSD, and the amphetamines ("speed") as well as to the incidence of their use. At least three patterns of middle-class drug use can be discerned. One pattern involves the use of drugs in a setting that is "delinquent," in the sense we have used the term in this book, in that drugs are used by groups of middle-class adolescents who are peer-oriented. The spending power provided by the favored economic and social position of middle-class youths makes drugs of various kinds accessible without the need—experienced by lower-class youths who use addictive narcotics—for gainful criminal activity. These youths face only a slight chance of being apprehended by police. In such delinquent groups, drug use may partially replace the use of alcohol by earlier generations.

It is quite likely that the impetus for the use of drugs by middle-class youths has come from the national publicity given the "hippie" movement of the middle and late 1960s.[27] While a full and objective analysis has yet to be made of the hippies, we can suggest three underlying factors that have probably contributed to the development of their movement. The first is a continuing "underground" tradition among some young, American intellectuals that has been transformed from bohemianism of the 30s to the "beat generation" of the 1950s to the present hippie movement. It is not difficult, as Bennett M. Berger has suggested,[28] to trace the moral ideals of the hippie— self-expression, pagan body worship, living for the moment, liberty, female equality, and mind-expansion, among others—to the earlier ideas of bohemianism. There is also evidence of some continuity of membership between the beat generation and hippies.[29] The second element is an apparently heightened sense of alienation from the values of middle-class America on the part of many middle-class youths, an alienation perhaps deepened by the twin events of a widely disliked war in Vietnam and the domestic situation of black Americans. The underlying root of alienation—the inability to construct a self of which one can be proud on the basis of the dominant values of the society—has clearly worked in conjunction with these events to produce an especially uncommitted group of youths. The third element is the ability of middle-class youths to construct —partly with the help of the mass media and the guidance of their older prophets—an ideology useful in organizing and justifying their desire to "turn on, tune in, and drop out."

The hippie movement, which received widespread public attention for a relatively short period of time, constitutes the second major pattern of drug use among middle-class adolescents. The use of drugs in that movement is a regular, everyday occurrence that is justified, and even demanded, by those in the hippie "culture."

The third—and least homogeneous—pattern of drug use exists on college and university campuses, where it represents neither middle-class, peer-group delinquency nor an especially pronounced allegiance to the hippie ideology. Instead, a number of groups within the university use drugs more or less regularly.[30] Some are political activists for whom drug use is not a central preoccupation, although it may be used socially, much as alcohol is, or in connection with an ideology of social and political revolution. Others are alienated from university life for a variety of reasons and find experimentation with drugs, sex, and alcohol a way of expressing dissatisfactions. They may retreat, although probably for a relatively short duration, to the life styles and ideologies of the hippie movement, but still retain their campus connections.[31] Still others use marijuana as a substitute for alcohol, with no other political or ideological involvements. On the campus generally, the publicity given the ideology and behavior of hippies has probably helped to provide color and form in the social rituals associated with drug use.

These patterns of drug use illustrate the advantageous position of middle-class youths. Middle-stratum delinquents who use drugs are probably less likely to be caught than lower-stratum juveniles are, although the public response to middle-class juvenile drug use has been more concerned than their reaction to lower-stratum narcotics addiction. Perhaps this may be partially explained by the fact that the cherished public image of clean, law-abiding, middle-class youths has been tarnished. Moreover, middle-class youths themselves have been able to manage their misdeeds far more to their own advantage than lower-stratum delinquents have. They have been able to surround their violations of the law with rather elaborate ideological defenses. Indeed, the evidence suggests that middle-class youths —when they become alienated from the values of the society and find it impossible to define themselves comfortably in conventional terms—are able to escape the unproductive, delinquency-prone orientations of lower-stratum youths and develop ideologies and organizations of *rebellion* instead.

The student protest movements of recent years, for example, have been largely composed of middle-class young people. It can be argued that the advantaged position of middle-class youths, with respect to both resources and personal skills, has enabled them to derive self-esteem from the pursuit of an activist orientation toward the society. Because middle-class youths do not suffer the severe psychological damage sustained by lower-stratum youths, their cognitive and interpersonal skills are sufficient to permit them the luxury of ideology and organization. But what is both perplexing and highly significant is that the social and political activism of many middle-class students does not stem from their inability to meet the dominant middle-class emphasis on achievement, since activists are often among the best students.

How, then, can their alienation be explained? Why is it that youths who have been very successful in conventional middle-class terms seem to reject middle-class values? Protesting youths themselves would explain their alienation in terms of what they regard as the evils of the society as presently constituted. But the sociologist must delve more deeply into the nature of the society to find an adequate explanation. Societies, one could argue, are always evil, but they are only rarely regarded so as vehemently by significant numbers of their young members as ours is at present.

One tentative hypothesis is that in families that have achieved stable middle-class standing socialization is more likely to be characterized by parental achievement than by the children's aspirations. In such families, youths are likely to perceive serious dissonance on a number of levels. They may very well contrast their parents' achievements with their perceptions (realistic or not) of their own chances of matching them. They will see, in an era of nearly instant diffusion of information, clear contrasts between the liberal ideology of middle-class American society and the harsh realities of poverty and injustice. They will perhaps see contrasts between the enormous power of modern technology as opposed to poverty, starvation, environmental pollution, and the preoccupation with technique and efficiency. Those who are most aware, in short, may see the dissonance between what is around them and the values they are taught. They may feel that if they were to conform to the social conventions of their parents, they would not be able to maintain self-respect, and they may see in various forms of political and social protest (whether focused on war, the conduct of the university, or sexual mores) a means of resolving this dissonance and of gaining self-esteem.

Status Crystallization and Self-Esteem

The middle-stratum ideology of prestige is threatening, at least potentially, to the self-esteem even of those who support it and fare well by it. The self-evaluations encouraged by the ideology may not match the evaluations that some people receive in contexts of social interaction. Although the main criteria of occupation, income, and education may encourage those with substantial achievements in these terms to think well of themselves and to expect deference from others, they may actually receive negative evaluations and suffer low prestige if they are members of low-rated racial, religious, or ethnic groups. And at specific levels of ethnic, racial, or religious status, some people will receive inconsistent or unexpected evaluations and prestige ratings because they stand on different rungs of other ladders (income, occupation, and education). The members of any stratified society tend to claim prestige according to criteria that assign them the highest prestige. Because the three major criteria do not correlate perfectly, however, we should expect some members of the society to receive evaluations that differ from those they expect. Disparities between educational and occupational rank, for example, might be especially significant because educational requirements have been upgraded in many occupations, so that some older practitioners could not meet the educational requirements for current entrants. In addition, although education is required for entrance into higher-stratum occupations, it is not a guarantee of success in them. It is interesting that Gerhard E. Lenski's initial empirical work, which related political attitudes to status crystallization (the condition in which a person occupies corresponding levels on several ladders of evaluation), revealed that the inconsistencies discussed here (occupation versus education and achievement versus ascriptive criteria) were the two most significantly related to political liberalism.[32]

What consequences of inconsistent evaluations can we predict? The self-esteem theory suggests that, to the extent that self-esteem depends upon prestige evalutions, inconsistent evaluations threaten it. More specifically, those who are exposed to such inconsistencies will attempt to withdraw from the contexts of social interaction in which the lowest evaluations are received, and their attitudes will reflect their anxieties about prestige. For middle-stratum people of low status crystallization voluntary associations related to the role of citizen are likely sources of inconsistent evaluations. That such people are likely to withdraw from or to participate less actively in such associations is supported by empirical evidence.[33]

The self-esteem model suggests that empirical research into status crystallization concentrate on disparities between the self-identifications by members of a society and the contradictory evaluations to which they are likely to be subjected. Individuals must resolve these disparities. Considerably more research is necessary in order to determine more precisely how such resolutions are made, as well as the conditions under which they lead to deviant behavior.

One interesting point remains. To the extent that the ideology of prestige is vague on specific gradations, all members of society, even the middle-stratum people who support the ideology, will face status inconsistencies at one time or another. The result may be widespread status anxiety, in which men strive for prestige under conditions of uncertainty—not only uncertainty about its attainment but also about its definition. Thomas Luckmann and Peter Berger have put it this way: "If status is relatively uncertain and relatively inconsistent, conditions are created that are unfavorable for the consistency and stability of the self."[34] Luckmann and Berger suggest that the widespread status anxiety thus created should be regarded as a crucial factor underlying many kinds of aberrant behavior, especially that arising from mental illness. The theory of self-esteem supports this point of view.

Notes

1. For a discussion of the difficulties attending the measurement of class and stratum see Harold M. Hodges, Jr., *Social Stratification: Class in America* (Cambridge, Mass.: Schenkman, 1964), pp. 39–101. For a discussion of elites see Suzanne Keller, *Beyond the Ruling Class* (New York: Random House, 1963).
2. See E. Digby Baltzell, *Philadelphia Gentlemen* (New York: Free Press, 1958).
3. For a discussion of the particular subcultures that make up the middle stratum and of the value differences between them, see Herbert Gans, *The Urban Villagers* (New York: Free Press, 1962), Chapter 11.
4. Bernard C. Rosen, "The Achievement Syndrome: A Psychocultural Dimension of Social Stratification," *American Sociological Review, 21* (1956), 203–211; Rosen, "Race, Ethnicity and the Achievement Syndrome," *American Sociological Review, 24* (1959), 47–60; and R. G. D'Andrade, "The Psychosocial Origins of Achievement Motivation," *Sociometry, 22* (1959), 185–218.
5. See, for example, C. Wright Mills, *White Collar* (New York: Oxford, 1951), pp. 239–258.
6. See Rosen, "The Achievement Syndrome."
7. See Rosen, "Race, Ethnicity and the Achievement Syndrome."
8. Harry J. Crockett, "Achievement Motivation and Differential Occupational Mobility in the U. S.," *American Sociological Review, 27* (1962), 193.
9. See David C. McClelland, *The Achieving Society* (Princeton, N.J.: Van Nostrand, 1961), pp. 340 ff. Also see J. W. Atkinson, ed., *Motives in Fantasy, Action and Society* (Princeton, N.J.: Van Nostrand, 1958).
10. Rosen, "The Achievement Syndrome," Table 6, p. 210.
11. Crockett, *op. cit.*
12. Robert J. Kleiner and Seymour Parker, "Goal-Striving, Social Status and Mental Disorder: A Research Review," *American Sociological Review, 28* (1963), 189–203.
13. Abraham Kardiner and L. Ovesey, *The Mark of Oppression* (New York: Norton, 1951), Chapter 9.
14. A. B. Hollingshead, R. Ellis, and E. Kirby, "Social Mobility and Mental Illness," *American Sociological Review, 19* (1954), 577–584.
15. Jerome K. Myers, and Bertram H. Roberts, *Family and Class Dynamics in Mental Illness* (New York: Wiley, 1959), pp. 133–137.
16. See especially Leo Srole, *et al., Mental Health in the Metropolis: The Midtown Manhattan Study* (New York: McGraw-Hill, 1962).

17. Albert K. Cohen, "Middle-Class Delinqency and the Social Structure," in Edmund W. Vaz, ed., *Middle-Class Juvenile Delinquency* (New York: Harper, 1967), pp. 203–207.

18. See Richard L. Simpson, "Parental Influence, Anticipatory Socialization and Social Mobility," *American Sociological Review*, 27 (1962), 517–522.

19. See A. J. Reiss and A. L. Rhodes, "The Distribution of Juvenile Delinquency in the Social Class Structure," *American Sociological Review*, 26 (1961), 732.

20. *Ibid.*, Table 1, p. 723.

21. *Ibid.*

22. See Cohen's chapter on juvenile delinquency in Robert K. Merton and Robert A. Nisbet, eds., *Contemporary Social Problems* (rev. ed; New York: Harcourt, 1966).

23. For a useful discussion of middle-class delinquency see Theodore N. Ferdinand, *Typologies of Delinquency* (New York: Random House, 1966).

24. Talcott Parsons, "Certain Primary Sources and Patterns of Aggression in the Social Structure of the Western World," *Psychiatry*, 10 (1947), 167–181.

25. Cohen, *Delinquent Boys* (New York: Free Press, 1955), p. 164.

26. For a discussion of the limited evidence now available see Richard H. Blum, "Mind Altering Drugs and Dangerous Behavior," in S. Dinitz, R. Dynes, and A. Clarke, eds., *Deviance* (New York: Oxford, 1969), pp. 280–291.

27. For one account, of uncertain objectivity, of the hippie phenomenon see Lewis Yablonsky, *The Hippie Trip* (New York: Pegasus, 1968). The book is richly descriptive but less carefully analytical than one would desire.

28. Bennett M. Berger, "Hippie Morality—More Old Than New," *Transaction*, 5 (December, 1967), 19–27. Berger's analysis is intuitive to some degree, but careful.

29. A useful discussion of the hippie movement emphasizing "the Diggers" is Fred Davis, "Why All of Us May be Hippies Someday," *Transaction*, 5 (December, 1967), 10–18.

30. Geoffrey Simon & Grafton Trout, "Hippies in College—From Teeny-boppers to Drug Freaks," *Transaction*, 5 (December, 1967), 27–32.

31. *Ibid.*

32. Gerhard E. Lenski, "Status-Crystallization: A Non-Vertical Dimension of Social Status," *American Sociological Review*, 19 (1954), 405–413.

33. Lenski, "Social Participation and Status Crystallization," *American Sociological Review*, 21 (1956), 458–464.

34. Thomas Luckmann and Peter Berger, "Social Mobility and Personal Identity," *European Journal of Sociology*, 5 (1964), 335.

The Social Implications of Inequality and Deviance

6

In this final chapter we shall attempt to summarize our analysis and to examine its social implications, raising and attempting to answer a series of important social and sociological questions.

The Long-Term Consequences of Deviant Behavior

What impact does deviant behavior have on a society? Do serious forms of deviant behavior, such as crime, have only negative consequences, or do they also make positive contributions to social well-being? If so, what kind of contributions do they make? Do various forms of protest, viewed as a special kind of deviance, constitute a threat to a society, or do they perform a valuable service by making it possible to adjust to changes in its own structure? Does low social participation threaten or help to guarantee the stability of the social order?

These questions are deceptively easy. Of course, one could reply, deviant behavior has only negative consequences for a society. It means that some members of the society are not involved in the performance of important social roles; it creates tensions and conflicts; it renders some individual lives miserable and wasted; it is costly in terms of the protection society requires from deviant members and that deviant members require from society and from themselves (prisons, mental institutions, police and legal apparatus, and the like); in the family it interferes with the socialization of new members of the society and thus reduces their ability to make their way in life; and it reduces the fully democratic operation of the society and helps to perpetuate social inequalities.

Yet, although deviant behavior is clearly costly for a society, it can also be argued that just about any form of deviant behavior has some *positive* consequences for society as well. As Melvin Tumin has demonstrated, it is not yet possible to measure the positive and negative contributions of any social arrangement to society as a whole.[1] We can specify some of the system-sustaining and system-destroying effects of various social arrangements, including deviant behavior, but we cannot add them up and arrive at a simple index of their overall influence. Nor can we, it must also be admitted, predict all the social consequences for society of particular forms of deviant behavior. In view of these problems, we can only suggest some possible positive contributions of deviant behavior.

What merits can be claimed, for example, for low social participation (defined as deviant behavior because it deviates from middle-stratum definitions of the role of the citizen)? The answer depends partly upon the theory of politics one accepts as valid for a pluralistic society. Pluralism refers to the existence of several competing groups within a society, each competing with the others to gain its objectives. Such groups may be regional, ethnic, religious, class, racial, and so forth. One could argue that low social participation deprives a society of the full scope of pluralistic competition. Members of some social strata do not participate fully in the organizational and political life of the society, and society also loses because the competitive process is unbalanced and because the special insights and contributions of these strata are lost. On the other hand, one can argue that it is not the nonparticipation of some groups that works against the pluralistic system but rather the attempts of middle-stratum groups to define competition solely in terms advantageous to them. A positive view of this form of deviance would imply that limited social participation helps to guarantee the stability of the democratic social order. If participation in politics and voluntary associations were to become active and total, it might be argued, the political system, at least as it is presently constituted, would become unstable, for government would become too cumbersome and previous nonparticipants might be unwilling to abide by present rules of political action. The difficulty of weighing the positive and negative contributions of low social participation becomes readily apparent.

Crime can be more clearly and conventionally defined as deviant. It is not difficult to demonstrate that crimes against property, people, and society are damaging to society, both materially and psychically. Yet it can also be argued that the social reaction to crime, which typically is moral indignation and outrage, promotes internal solidarity and reduces dissent.[2] The violation of social norms provides an opportunity for the norms to be reaffirmed through the punishment of the offender. It is impossible to say, and perhaps not even meaningful to ask, whether the positive effects of moral solidarity outweigh the negative effects of theft, for example, because we cannot easily add up the short- and long-range benefits of the reaffirmation of rights to property and then measure them against injury to the rights of specific people.

And what of the protest movements that have become a common feature of American life? They certainly constitute deviance from the standpoint of many Americans, for they strike at what many would regard as the roots of the society: its underlying economic and political orientations and even its code of sexual conduct. Yet it can also be argued that such rebellious deviance is all to the society's benefit, that it strikes at many of the deepest roots of dissatisfaction and alienation in the society—bureaucratic impersonality, a sense of powerlessness, racial and economic inequality, and militarism. Even passive drop-outs from the society, whether assigned the magic status of "hippies" by the mass media or not, may contribute positively to the society by dramatizing what they regard as the necessity and the possibility of dropping out.

We must also be alert to the fact that there are usually alternatives for the satisfaction of certain functional conditions in a society. For example, if we say that political stability and moral solidarity are beneficial to society, we have left entirely open the question of how such conditions are to be attained. Presumably there are alternative social arrangements that could meet these conditions. There are many forms of government, including perhaps some in which stability is promoted by widespread, rational participation in politics and government. Moral solidarity may be better ensured by widespread cultural uniformity or by the absence of inequalities that promote dissension than by moral solidarity in response to deviance.

One simple measure of the effects of deviant behavior on society is the Gross National Product. To the extent that it is increased by various forms of deviant behavior, we could say that deviance contributes positively to the society; to the extent that it is reduced that deviance contributes negatively. Although crime is frequently businesslike and very beneficial to those who control it, the total effect of deviant behavior on the production of goods and services is negative. Societies must expend considerable resources to maintain prisons, mental institutions, and police forces; these resources do not contribute to productivity. Furthermore, some forms of deviant behavior actually subtract from productivity: Mental illness prevents social roles from being performed as fully or productively as possible, and because the prevalence of mental disorder in the population is probably far more widespread than is suggested by the number of people who are institutionalized such losses are probably quite severe.[3] Family disorganization may have effects similar to those of mental disorder, in reducing motivation, threatening morale, and contributing to imperfect socialization of new generations. Juvenile delinquency also interrupts the socialization process and reduces the ability of former delinquents to participate successfully in the labor market. It is clear, then, that deviant behavior reduces society's economic productivity.

But limiting the concept of productivity to goods and services means omission of other kinds of satisfactions, which are much more difficult to analyze.

Societies can be relatively easily compared in terms of their economic outputs, but what of the other gratifications that they afford their members? It is difficult to decide whether or not there are any uniform standards by which such gratifications can be assessed. Perhaps good health comes closer to a universal standard than does any other value. But security, peace, excitement, risk, fulfillment, truth, justice, and other values are defined and rated very differently in various societies—or even within one society—and it is not the task of the sociologist to say what ought and what ought not to be *socially* important. The concept of self-esteem, however, provides a measure of psychic satisfactions that may well be sufficiently universal to provide comparisons of psychic productivity among societies and among alternative social arrangements within the same society.

We have asserted that the need for self-esteem is universal and that, whatever the specific social arrangements and cultural values, men use them to define the kind of people they themselves are and ought to be. The consequences of being unable to develop adequate self-esteem include low commitment to society and its norms, high levels of anxiety, and high likelihood of involvement in various forms of deviant behavior. Nevertheless social arrangements are structured so that some members of society are prevented from developing adequate self-esteem. In any society some members will thus be prevented from obtaining psychic rewards, however the specific rewards are defined. If we adopt the simple measure of counting the members of any society, or of any social group, who develop adequate self-esteem (who feel sufficiently well-disposed toward themselves to avoid the paralyzing effects of anxiety), we have a measure of the degree to which society and its arrangements produce psychic gratifications.

Viewed in this light, deviant behavior not only affects material productivity itself but also serves as a channel through which social inequality in turn affects material productivity. Obstacles to adequate self-esteem arising from social inequality and uncongenial ideologies of prestige are certainly not the only cause of deviant behavior, but they are clearly a major factor in many forms. The ultimate cause of deviant behavior and its dysfunctional consequences must thus be viewed as largely dependent upon social inequality.

The Future of Inequality and Equality

If we accept the premise that social inequality is the ultimate source of many inadequacies in self-esteem, of deviant behavior, and of reduced social productivity, then we must answer two additional questions. First, to what extent is it possible for a society to reduce social inequality? And, second, to what degree must adequate self-esteem depend upon the possibility of reducing inequality? The answers are difficult.

To some extent the issue of reducing inequalities has been solved in western industrial democracies, and the question is more empirical than theoretical in those societies. As T. H. Marshall has pointed out,[4] the history of industrialism in the West has been marked by progressive incorporation of larger and wider segments of these societies into a common network of legal norms, rights, processes, and obligations. Increasingly, industrial societies attempt to cope with the welfare of their members by insuring them against the hazards of old age, disability, and unemployment; by making the legal apparatus of the state available to all; and by extending the role of the citizen to all members of the society. In other words, the tendency has been to ensure all members of the society certain minimum life chances. To claim total success would be absurd, as our eyes and ears readily testify, but inequalities in life chances have been significantly reduced.

What of the future? Can remaining material inequalities be reduced to the point at which *all* members of society share at least minimum standards of health, education, family stability, and the like? The recent experience of the United States suggests that the eradication of "hard core" poverty is difficult, but not only because it is a major task to redirect and re-energize the motives and skills of the poor, but also because it is politically difficult to mobilize the resources needed to do so. The future of material inequality in this regard thus depends upon time and money, both of which—to judge from the recent bitter juxtaposition of racial conflict and foreign war—may well be scarce. But what of inequality in general? Social inequality has generated considerable theoretical controversy, particularly over the functional necessity of social inequality. In 1945 Wilbert E. Moore and Kingsley Davis argued that social inequality—in the form of unequal material and prestige rewards for occupations —is necessary in order for a society to guarantee that its most competent and talented members will fill the most difficult and important positions.[5] Those who undertake long periods of training and difficult and important tasks must be rewarded for their special efforts. The major assumption about motivation on which this theory is based—universal agreement that it is just to receive unequal rewards for unequal efforts—also consti- tutes its major difficulty. It is not difficult to demonstrate, of course, that such a notion of justice prevails publicly in indus- trial societies. We should not, however, accept without question the premise that this particular concept of distributive justice, and the motivational arrangements it reflects, is universal and inevitable.

The Moore-Davis theory assumes that men will be willing to engage in difficult and demanding activities only if they re- ceive special recognition, in the form of prestige and material rewards, for their efforts. If we decide that such motivation is universal, then we must ask how unequal the rewards must be in order to motivate appropriately unequal performances.

Let us assume that a physician earns $30,000 a year and an assembly-line worker $7,500. According to the Moore-Davis theory the difference is necessary to ensure that enough talented men will be willing to devote their time and energies to the difficult training required to become a physician and to the demanding work that a physician must do. Factory work de- mands less training, and therefore, it is argued, factory workers can be more easily replaced and do not have to be paid as much.

But is it possible to find other ways to encourage the talented to develop their talents to the full? If some material inequalities are still necessary, how great must they be?

Could we equalize the material and prestige rewards of all occupations yet provide other rewards sufficient to motivate talented people to do demanding work? Such rewards might be based on an internal sense of satisfaction derived from performing social service. Perhaps men could be persuaded that membership in society entails the duty to develop talents to their fullest and to serve where their talents are most needed. Of course, the crucial issue is how motivation *can* be socially structured. The Moore-Davis theory assumes that men can be motivated only by extrinsic rewards for the tasks they perform and not by rewards intrinsic to the task itself or by the satisfactions of social interaction and a sense of service. But men behave within other spheres—like the family—without attention to the extrinsic rewards that they receive. Why not also in the work they do? There is no simple answer. We might also suggest that, if there must be inequalities among various occupations, then at least there could be some attempt to guarantee that every occupation would be rewarding in one way or another. If not well-paid, perhaps it could be intrinsically rewarding or provide rewarding interpersonal relationships. To what extent are such alternative motivational arrangements possible?

It is impossible to provide a conclusive answer, but the evidence suggests that at least some inequality is difficult to avoid, even though it has not been demonstrated that it is functionally necessary. Occupational tasks differ considerably in their characteristics, and, although it is possible to imagine a society in which unskilled manual work is perceived to be as intrinsically rewarding as is creative intellectual work, it seems difficult to bring about such a change in any existing society. To do so requires, as the example of the Israeli Kibbutżim perhaps shows, special conditions and energies.[6] Furthermore, there is the complex and difficult question of power, which heavily influences the distribution of rewards in society.

Much social inequality is best explained not by the importance or difficulty of occupational positions but by inequalities in the power associated with those positions. For instance, the factory worker and the physician differ in their respective power to determine their own incomes, as well as in the difficulty and the supposed importance of their work. Physicians set their own fees, whereas factory workers are employed at wages over which they have little or no individual control. The importance of power reminds us that the allocation of a society's resources among its members is not controlled by an automatic and impersonal process that calculates the precise rewards necessary to ensure the services of different people with different skills. Rather, the distribution of rewards is controlled by people with various degrees of power over their own compensation and that of others. Individuals vary, primarily along occupational lines, in their ability to make the market for their services bear what they would like it to bear. Their success depends upon the level of demand for their services in relation to the scarcity of supply; their ability to restrict supply by regulating access to the occupation; the extent to which there are alternative ways of meeting demand for their services; and many other factors. This suggests that, even though some inequality may be inevitable, the existing degrees and kinds of inequality may be far greater and more consequential than necessary.

The consequences of material inequalities do not, of course, depend solely upon their magnitude. They also arise from the extent to which life chances are dependent upon income. In Western societies, inequalities in income thus tend to have a less severe impact as certain basic life chances are gradually extended to all members of those societies as a matter of fundamental right. As we have indicated, however, the extension of such basic life chances as health and education has by no means been completed. Furthermore the improvement of life chances, regardless of income, cannot be taken as all that is required to eliminate or reduce the impact of inequality upon self-esteem.

It is, of course, true that poor life chances tend to undermine self-esteem, for those who are materially least well off must daily confront the bitter evidence of their failure to measure up to society's material standards of success. A man who cannot provide for the simplest material wants of his family finds it difficult to see himself as manly and worthy, at least in American society, which places the blame for failure squarely upon the individual. Poor life chances both cause and confirm low self-esteem. But the sense of deprivation that leads to low self-esteem is based on a relative standard, rather than upon absolute notions of success or failure. People feel deprived not simply in absolute terms but, more important, in terms of their misery relative to their perception of the standard of living enjoyed by others. Therefore, if conditions are improved for all without changes in relative standing, those who are most deprived relative to the rest will continue to feel injured.

Not that a sense of material deprivation relative to the rest of the society is sufficient in itself to produce low self-esteem. In American society, two other factors operate to magnify the effects of material inequalities. They are, first, differential evaluation of positions and attributes and, second, the existence of social arrangements that simultaneously emphasize the importance of prestige and lessen alternative means of building self-esteem.

First, although there is no evidence that differential evaluation is functionally necessary, it remains as an important fact. Some positions are valued more highly than others, and some attributes—education, ethnic affiliation, race, religion—either command respect or not. Differential evaluation of positions and attributes also tends to become embedded in the ideologies of prestige that people espouse in diverse contexts of interaction. Material inequalities that do exist are explained by these ideologies in terms of value and social worth, and those who are not materially well off are under considerable pressure to attribute their failure to their own lack of effort or merit.

Second, inequalities in material rewards and social evaluation mesh with features of the social structure that make creation and maintenance of alternative value systems very difficult. Those who are most deprived materially and in terms of evaluations from others can find no really secure retreat from the ideology that devalues them. For lower-stratum members of American society, the effects of low income and low prestige are multiplied by this difficulty. The fortunate working-class person finds that the price of self-esteem is retreat into a family life, where immunity from unfavorable evaluations can be guaranteed. Less fortunate members of the lower class, however, find that poor life chances and low self-esteem have established a treadmill, at the center of which is the disorganized family. The stratification system promotes family disorganization, and members of the lower class very often cannot turn to their families in refuge from the system of material and psychic inequalities. For those lower-stratum people who become oriented toward social mobility into the middle stratum and for those middle-stratum individuals who take the ideology of prestige especially seriously, self-esteem comes to depend upon success as defined by the ideology; devotion to upward mobility is therefore likely to intensify patterns of behavior conventionally classified as resulting from mental disorder.

The prospects for future equality, therefore, appear bleak. The social consequences of social inequality—lowered morale, imperfect socialization, and deviant behavior of many kinds— themselves operate to reinforce patterns of inequality. Social inequality and its consequences form a system of recurring variables, and the crucial (and unanswered) questions are related to points at which the system can most efficiently be changed.

Culture For and Against Man

In our analysis we have attempted to demonstrate why the conventional image of man's cultural and social arrangements as promoting his physical and psychic survival is not completely accurate. To borrow from the title of a recent book by Jules Henry,[7] culture frequently works *against* man, rather than for him. We have argued that cultural arrangements requiring men to evaluate one another and social arrangements in which power and material resources are unequally distributed work against man by making full, normative, and productive participation in the social order difficult and often impossible.

To be sure, social inequalities are not the only social and cultural arangements that work against human interests, nor is deviant behavior the sole relevant measure of how well or ill those interests are served. But social stratification is perhaps the most powerful single variable in the explanation of behavioral variations within a society, and deviant behavior provides the clearest index of a society's ability to live with its own norms. It is for these reasons that we have emphasized their interrelations in this analysis.

In Conclusion

In this book we have expressed the view that to explain behavior we must take account of individual factors that cause it—motives, attitudes, abilities, personality dispositions, and the like—as well as of social structures, which not only provide limitations and opportunities for individuals but also play dominant roles in determining their psychological character-istics. That is, men's behavior is not simply a result of their motives or other internal characteristics; it is also a product of the social situations in which they find themselves.

In our analysis of stratification and deviant behavior, for example, we argued that men seek to develop self-esteem by participating in various social relationships and by adhering to their norms. But deviant behavior (or conforming behavior) is not simply a product of this striving for self-esteem; it is a joint product of the striving and the social arrangements in which the striving is carried on. The delinquent boy is delinquent not simply because he has found it difficult to construct adequate self-esteem but also because the conditions in which he is forced to seek self-esteem—mainly in the company of his peers—make violations of the law and conflict with law-enforcement agencies probable. We therefore say that behavior is a joint product of individual dispositions and social structure.[8]

In focusing upon individual dispositions, we have used the concept of self-esteem as a strategic device for discussing the relationships between individual and society. We have adopted the view that the construction of a social identity is central to the behavior in which a person engages and that it is crucially important that he approve the result. The ability to assert and approve one's own identity, however, depends upon the actions and reactions of people and situations external to the individual. Self-esteem thus provides the critical links between internal disposition, external social constraints, and behavior.

Not that all behavior is capable of explanation in terms of a single variable, however. The concept of self-esteem is useful, not because it replaces other concepts, but because it helps to organize them. Concepts like identity, self-image, motivation, anxiety, goals, commitments, norms, and values can be organized and related to one another through the strategic concept of self-esteem. Our reliance on self-esteem does not imply that it is a more significant goal than success or security, for example. But the goals men seek, the socially approved motives they develop, the norms to which they become committed, their abilities, and the behavior they exhibit are strategically interrelated. Self-esteem is not a goal that competes with other goals for men's attention; rather it operates at a fundamental level to direct those other goals and the motives, abilities, and behavior they entail.

Notes

1. Melvin Tumin, "The Functionalist Approach to Social Problems," *Social Problems*, 12 (1965), 379–388.
2. See the classic work by Emile Durkheim, *The Division of Labor in Society* (New York: Free Press, 1964).
3. See Leo Srole, *et al.*, *Mental Health in the Metropolis: The Midtown Manhattan Study* (New York: McGraw-Hill, 1962), Chapter 8. Some idea of the magnitude of the loss to society of the talents and energies of its members can be gained from the number of people confined in institutions for mental illness and in prisons. The average daily adult prison population in the U. S. is well over 350,000, and in 1964 the total population in all types of mental institutions was about 565,000, for a total of over 900,000 adults. (See Marshall B. Clinard, *The Sociology of Deviant Behavior* (3rd ed.; New York: Holt, 1968), pp. 784–804.) In addition to the cost required to maintain such a large institutionalized population, the loss in total productivity (assuming a per capita income of $2,800) is on the order of at least two and one-half billion dollars per year.
4. See T. H. Marshall, *Class, Citizenship and Social Development* (New York: Doubleday Anchor, 1965).
5. Wilbert E. Moore and Kingsley Davis, "Some Principles of Stratification," *American Sociological Review*, 10 (1945), 242–249. For a response to the theory see Tumin, "Some Prin-

ciples of Stratification: A Critical Analysis," *American Socio-logical Review, 18* (1953), 387–394.

6. See Melford E. Spiro, *Children of the Kibbutz* (Cambridge, Mass.: Harvard University Press, 1958).

7. Jules Henry, *Culture Against Man* (New York: Random House, 1963). This book is highly recommended.

8. For a presentation of a field-theoretical point of view see J. Milton Yinger, *Toward a Field Theory of Behavior* (New York: McGraw-Hill, 1965). Field theory, as Yinger discusses it, seeks to bring the individual and the social structure together. Individual behavior is explained by the intersection of personality variables that are internal to the individual and situational factors that derive from social structure. Much of this book is field theoretical in that sense.

Index

Family (*continued*)
  class and stratum differences
    in role of, 53–55
  disorganization in, 55, 111–
    112, 115–117
  obstacles to self-esteem in, 42–
    43, 58–61
  relationship to delinquency,
    89–92
Feldman, Arnold, 28n
Ferdinand, Theodore N., 154n
Festinger, Leon, 131n
Field theory, 168n
Floud, Jean, 103n
Form, William H., 28n

Gangs, delinquent, 75, 80, 81–
  82, 144
Gans, Herbert, 53, 102n, 153n
Gerth, Hans, 35, 49n
Gibbons, Don C., 105n
Glazer, Nathan, 28n
Glueck, Sheldon and Eleanor, 89,
  105n
Goffman, Erving, 28n
Goldstein, Leo, 103n
Gordon, Robert A., 104n
Griswold, Manzer J., 105n
Gross, Llewellyn, 28n
Gross National Product, 158
Groups: and normative behavior,
  7–9
  delinquent, experiences in, 93–
    96
  peer, and self-esteem, 46–47
Guilt and internalized norms, 6–7
Gursslin, Orville R., 49n
Gyman, Harry, 132n

Halsey, A. H., 103n
Hartly, Eugene L., 102n
Hempel, Carl G., 28n
Henry, Jules, 165, 168n
Himmelhoch, Jerome, 104n
Hinkle, Lawrence E., 126, 132n
Hippies, 148
Hodge, Robert W., 130n

Hodges, Harold M., Jr., 102n,
  130n, 153n
Hokanson, Jack E., 131n
Hollingshead, August B., 126,
  131n, 132n, 141, 153n
Hyman, Herbert, 130n

Ideal/actual discrepancies and
  prestige, 23, 26–27
Income: as criterion of evaluation, 25
  and the lower class, 56–57
Inequality: as socially structured,
  14–15
  effects on self-esteem summa-
    rized, 48, 163–165
  functional necessity of, 18,
    160–163
Inkeles, Alex, 29n
Interaction, context of: and prestige bargaining, 18–23
  definition of, 15
  delinquent groups as, 94–96
Internalization: definition of, 6
  relationship to commitment,
    6–7
Interpersonal relationships: and
  mental illness, 121, 124,
  141
  and self-esteem, 37–38
  in delinquent groups, 94–96

John, Vera P., 103n
Juvenile delinquency, lower-stratum: and family experi-
  ences, 89–92
  and delinquent group, 93–96
  as solution to delinquents
    problems, 93–96
  attitudes of delinquents to, 93–
    94, 95, 97–98
  critique of other theories, 80–
    87
  effects of treatment, 127–129
  precipitating factors in, 96–97
  reform from, 87, 98–99, 127–
    128

Merton, Robert K., 26, 29n, 102n, 104n, 130n, 131n, 132n, 154n
Middle class: definition of, 134–135
values of and delinquency, 83
Middle stratum: and status crystallization, 151–152
behavioral orientations in, 137–138
definition of, 133–134
delinquency in, 142–149
drug use in, 147–149
importance of achievement in, 136–137
mental illness in, 141–142
relationship to lower-stratum, 51–52, 53–54
relationship to upper stratum, 134–135; role of family in, 53–54
student protest in, 149–151
Miller, Herman, 57, 102n
Miller, S. M., 54, 102n
Mills, C. Wright, 35, 49n, 153n
Minnesota Multiphasic Personality Inventory, 114
Moore, Wilbert, 18, 28n
Motivation: and the explanation of deviance, 12–14
as component of the self, 32
to construct self-esteem, 35–37
Moynihan, Daniel P., 102n, 112, 130n
Murray, Elen, 105n
Myers, Jerome K., 126, 132n, 141, 153n

n Ach: see Achievement motivation
National Opinion Research Center, 29n
Negroes: and caste sanctions, 113–114
and family disorganization, 115–117
and mental illness, 112–115

and welfare, 111–112
and support for militancy, 117–120
Neuroses, 122
Neutralization, techniques of: definition of, 86
empirical study of, 93–94
in middle-stratum delinquency, 145–146
Newcomb, Theodore M., 102n
New Haven, 126
Niederhoffer, Arthur, 80, 104n
Nisbet, Robert A., 102n, 104n, 130n, 131n, 132n, 154n
Norms: and personal and social controls, 7–8
and the definition of deviant behavior, 11–13
commitment of delinquents to, 84–87, 93–95, 147
commitment to and self-esteem, 37
commitment to and the self, 32
definition of, 5
internalization of, 6
Nye, F. Ivan, 76, 77, 90, 91, 104n, 105n

Occupation: and prestige in American society, 25
as a basis for stratifying American society, 51–52, 133–134
Ohlin, Lloyd, 81, 82, 87, 104n
O'Neal, Patricia, 132n
Ovesey, Lionel, 112, 131n, 141, 153n

Parker, Seymour, 114, 126, 131n, 132n, 141, 153n
Parsons, Talcott, 28n, 146, 154n
Passow, A. Harry, 103n
Peers: and behavioral orientations, 65–66, 68, 69, 138
and the pursuit of self-esteem, 71–73

Peers (*continued*)
    as a context of socialization,
        42, 46–57, 85, 88
    definition of, 41
    promotion of anxieties by, 95–
        96
Personality disorders, 122–123
Philadelphia, 114
Poverty, 57–58
    and disrepute, 57, 131n
Power: and ideologies of prestige,
        19–20
    and inequalities of income,
        162–163
    and prestige bargaining, 18–22
    and voluntary associations, 109
    as means of behavioral control,
        9
    relation to authority, 9
    and definition of deviance, 10
Prestige: belief in by middle stra-
        tum, 134–135
    competition among ideologies
        of, 20–21
    conditions for consensus about,
        16–17
    definition of, 15
    ideal/actual discrepancies in
        allocation, 23, 26–27
    ideologies of, 19–25
    ideologies of in American so-
        ciety, 25–27, 134–135
    property as a criterion, 14
    stability and instability of, 24
Prestige bargaining, 18–25; defin-
        ition of, 21
    role of ideologies in, 18–21
    determinants of outcomes, 21–
        22
Protestant Ethic as a prestige
        ideology, 19
Psychoses, 122
Psychosomatic disorders, 122

Rainwater, Lee, 131n
Reckless, Walter, 76, 104n, 105n
Redlich, Frederick, 131n

Reiss, Albert J., Jr., 78, 79, 105n,
        154n
Religion and prestige, 27, 59
Retreatist delinquency, 75
Revolution and Negroes, 117–119
Rhodes, Albert L., 78, 79, 105n,
        154n
Riesman, David, 28n
Riessman, Frank, 54, 102n
Riots, urban, 117–119
Rivera, Ramon, 105n
Roach, Jack L., 49n
Roberts, Bertram H., 126, 132n
Robins, Lee N., 132n
Roles: definition of, 32
    and deviant behavior, 12–13
Rosen, Bernard, 138, 139, 140,
        153n
Rossi, Peter, 29

Scarpitti, Frank R., 105n
Schatzman, Leonard, 103n
School: obstacles to self-esteem
        in, 61–63
    as public context of socializa-
        tion, 41–42
Schwartz, Michael, 105n
Self: nature and composition of,
        32–33
    role in explanation of behavior,
        31
Self-concept and delinquency,
        101
Self-image: as a component of
        self, 33
    dimensions of, 33–34
Self-esteem: adequate level of de-
        fined, 38
    among the mobility-oriented,
        120–121, 141–142
    and anxiety, 38
    and autonomy, 36–37
    and black family structure,
        112, 115–117
    and broken homes, 59
    and commitments to norms, 37
    and fantasy, 36

Self-esteem *(continued)*
and interpersonal relationships, 37–38
and mental illness among blacks, 112–115
and religion, 59
and sex differences, 64
and social stratification, 47–48
and welfare, 111–112
as measure of psychic productivity, 159
definition of, 34
formation and behavioral import of, 34–40
in the delinquent group, 93–96
level of and social class, 58–61
motivation to develop, 35
obstacles for lower-class adults, 109–111
obstacles for lower-class Negroes, 111–120
obstacles for working-class adults, 108–109
obstacles in the family, 42–43
obstacles in lower-stratum families, 58–61
obstacles in public contexts, 44–45
obstacles in middle-stratum families, 136–138
obstacles in school, 61–63
pursuit among peers, 71–73
relationship to mental illness and mobility, 120–126, 140–142
Sexton, Patricia, 102n, 103n
Shame and commitment to norms, 7
Short, James F., 76, 77, 84, 104n, 105n, 132n
Significant others: and self-esteem, 35
limits on selection of, 35–36
definition of, 35
Simon, Geoffrey, 154n
Simpson, Richard L., 103n, 154n

Skipper, James K., 105n
Social adjustment and mental illness, 123
Social class: and delinquency rates, 76–80
and mental illness, 126–127
and level of self-esteem, 58–61
definition of, 54
Socialization: and the growth of self, 32
class differences in, 102n
important contexts of, 41–42
"normal" process of, 39–40
relationship to self-esteem summarized, 45–46
Social mobility: and American ideology of prestige, 26
and delinquency, 129
and mental illness, 120–127, 140–142
development of orientation to, 66–68
Social participation: and social class, 108–109
and status crystallization, 152
consequences of low, 156–157
Social stratification: definition of, 14
effects of self-esteem summarized, 47–48, 163–165
functional necessity of, 160–165
in American society, 25–27
Sounding in delinquent groups, 96
Spiro, Melford E., 168n
Srole, Leo, 125, 131n, 132n, 153n, 167n
Status crystallization and self-esteem, 150–152
Stone, Gregory P., 28n
Stratum: definition of, 14
Strauss, Anselm, 49n, 103n
Strodtbeck, Fred L., 84, 104n, 105n
Student protest, 149–151